Flip Thinking

FLIP
Thinking

The Life-Changing Art
of Turning Problems
into Opportunities

BERTHOLD GUNSTER

BALLANTINE BOOKS • NEW YORK

Copyright © 2023 by Berthold Gunster

All rights reserved.

Published in the United States by Ballantine Books, an imprint of Random House, a division of Penguin Random House LLC, New York.

BALLANTINE is a registered trademark and the colophon is a trademark of Penguin Random House LLC.

Originally published in Dutch in the Netherlands as *HUH?! De technick van het omdenken* by Levbocken, Amsterdam, in 2016. This translation, by Kelly Atkinson, was originally published in 2023 by Ebury Edge, an imprint of Ebury Publishing, a division of Penguin Random House UK, in 2023.

Library of Congress Cataloging-in-Publication Data
Names: Gunster, Berthold, author.
Title: Flip thinking: the life-changing art of turning problems into opportunities / Berthold Gunster.
Description: First edition. | New York, New York: Ballantine Group, 2023. Includes index. | Identifiers: LCCN 2023017775 (print) | LCCN 2023017776 (ebook) | ISBN 9780593723555 (hardcover) | ISBN 9780593723562 (ebook)
Subjects: LCSH: Thought and thinking. | Thought and thinking—Philosophy. | Conduct of life.
Classification: LCC BF441 .G86 2023 (print) | LCC BF441 (ebook) | DDC 153.4—dc23/eng/20230605
LC record available at https://lccn.loc.gov/2023017775
LC ebook record available at https://lccn.loc.gov/2023017776

Printed in the United States of America on acid-free paper

randomhousebooks.com

2 4 6 8 9 7 5 3 1

FIRST US EDITION

Book design by Ralph Fowler

Contents

PART 1
The Luggage

PART 2
The Journey

PART 3

Finally

Yes-but

Imagine this: you've got a great idea, and all you hear are the yes-buts. "Yes, but that's been tried before, and it didn't work." "Yes, but shouldn't we just let it sit for a while?" "Yes, but what if it doesn't work . . ."

All those yes-buts make you feel that every attempt at innovation will be buried in a swampy morass of seemingly sensible objections. And that's exactly how it works: yes-but thinking takes a closed attitude to life, throwing up restrictions and threats like dragons blocking your path. However worthwhile an idea or argument might be, it's met with rigidity, which leads to stagnation.

There's another way: the yes-and attitude. This open-minded perspective emphasizes what *can* be done, appreciating possibilities. With this attitude we see past the dragons to the path forward. The result? Creativity and innovation.

This book is about the transition from a yes-but to a yes-and way of living; from thinking in terms of problems to thinking in terms of opportunities. When we approach a problem with a yes-and mindset, novel solutions can sometimes be surprisingly easy to discover. Looking at a problem from a new angle, even just a quarter turn, can lead to a big insight, with so little effort. We don't have to fight our problems; we can *transform* them into opportunities. We can make them our allies.

The art of turning problems into opportunities can be learned. It's a type of psychological jujitsu, a technique that I call "Flip Thinking" (or *Omdenken* in my native Dutch). Flip thinking not only leads to a solution to an existing problem but, unexpectedly and surprisingly, it can open completely new vistas of possibility. As a caterpillar morphs into a butterfly, a problem is *flip-thought* into a beautiful new reality. This leads to a surprising paradox: the more problems we confront, the better.

At its core, flip thinking can improve your life, paradoxically enough, not by avoiding your problems, nor denying them by emphasizing only the good like a Pollyanna, but by embracing problems, recognizing and accepting pain, loss, and want. Flip thinking always starts with acknowledging reality. A pessimist is completely indifferent to how much water there is in the glass; he'll still just moan that he'll have to do the dishes again. Why not enjoy the glass of water instead?

I started the concept of flip thinking in the Netherlands, where I live, in 1997. Since then, my team of actors and trainers and I have put on more than 10,000 theatrical, entertaining, and educational workshops on the principles of flip thinking for, altogether, more than 1 million people. Besides performances in the Netherlands, a British–American team of actors and trainers performs flip-thinking sessions in Spain, Singapore, Britain, Germany, and France. In total, I have written 12 books about the principle of flip thinking, all of them bestsellers. In the Netherlands alone they have sold more than 1.3 million copies (bear in mind we have a population of only 17.4 million people!). These books have been translated into Italian, Portuguese, Danish, German and—as you are reading right now—English.

The story of flip thinking doesn't end here. It develops, grows, and matures. And I'm proud that you, dear reader, are a part of this journey. Hopefully you'll enjoy this book. Hopefully you'll take much away from it. Above all, I hope you'll come away from reading it with the understanding that problems are nothing more and nothing less than frustration that hasn't found its form yet. Frustration then can be enjoyed once it is flipped and transformed into a new, desirable, sparkling reality.

Berthold Gunster

Put this book on your bedside table

A few thoughts on how to read this book

First.

I once read that around 64 percent of people regularly read before going to sleep, that the average reading time is 10 minutes, and the average reading pace is around 300 words per minute. This may not be true for every reader, but with these averages in mind I divided this book into chapters of around 3,000 words each, so you can fit in a chapter each night before bed.

Second.

The book is not a novel; it's nonfiction. It describes thoughts, approaches, and (hopefully) inspiring examples of flip thinking. However, there's no such thing as "the theory of flip thinking" that I could set out from A to Z in a logical, straightforward instruction. Explaining to someone how to flip-think without letting them try it for themselves can perhaps best be compared to trying to give someone a tour of your house without being able to take them inside. By looking at it from the outside, perhaps through a window or the letterbox, or going around to a side door, or even peering down the chimney, you see something different each time, and along the way you (possibly) have the nagging feeling that you're missing the full experience. So I encourage you to not just take my word for it, but to step inside the house, get stuck in it, and apply flip thinking to your own life in order to really get a feel for it.

Third.

Learning takes place on multiple levels: some is conscious, but much is unconscious. We read something, dream about it, talk about it with someone the next day, and then often intuitively apply some insight gained, realizing only later that we have done so. This is another reason that I recommend reading at your leisure, bit by bit. Step by step, reading a chapter each day, you'll give your mind time to absorb, and delight in, the discoveries. You may also want to re-read some of the chapters at some point.*

Fourth.

Pay no attention to the three previous thoughts.

Read the book however you want. Or maybe not at all.

---

* Even though I've been writing and speaking about flip thinking for more than 15 years, I still often refer back to material I've introduced countless times. "This is interesting stuff, I really should do something with it!" Evidently there's an enormous gulf between understanding and doing.

Yes-but

**Thinking of what
should be,
but isn't.**

Yes-and

Seeing what's there, and what you could do with it.

Flip thinking

A pessimist sees the difficulty in every opportunity;
an optimist sees the opportunity in every difficulty.

Before we get started, let me tell you a bit more about my background. I trained as a theater director with a specialty in improvisation, or "improv" as it is commonly known. This background laid the foundation for my flip-thinking philosophy. What are the golden rules of improv? Two simple things. To *accept* reality as it is and to *do something* with it. Imagine an improv scene where one actor is a dentist and the other one is a patient. Would there be a scene where the patient did not present a problem? Well, it would be a dull scene: "Good morning," "Good morning," "How are you?," "I'm fine," "All right, see you next year," "Bye," "Bye." Improv, like all good drama, revolves around a problem. So what do improv actors learn? They learn to embrace or, even better, love problems and what can be created out of them. Use problems as the jumping-off point.

When I started working as a theater director I didn't follow the usual path. For more than ten years I created theater plays with and about people who experienced setbacks in life: people who lived in underserved neighborhoods in the city of Utrecht, who faced poverty, unemployment, and other social problems. I also worked with runaway kids, homeless people, and individuals dealing with addiction to drugs or alcohol. I created theater with these people not only in the Netherlands, but also in Ukraine, Spain, Scotland, Germany, Poland, Belgium, and the USA. In Chicago I initiated a project with homeless people called *Not Your Mama's Bus Tour.* During this theatrical bus tour, people who were homeless or formerly homeless showed the audience a glimpse of the city through the eyes of the homeless.

During all these theater projects as a director I had to learn one important thing: the people I worked with were not trained as professional actors. Though many of them had undisputed natural theatrical skills, I was forced to work within a lot of limitations. So what did I have to do? I had to learn to work like an improv actor: accept reality as it is, see and accept the limitations of my "actors," and at the same time discover what abilities they do have and how I can make genuine, convincing, authentic theater with them as they are, not as I hope they might be. So flip thinking was unavoidable. What can you do when five television stations want to cover the opening night of a play with homeless people—one of them being CNN—but one of the actors doesn't show up? You can be angry, frustrated, or disappointed, but these emotions will not help the problem. Only flip thinking does. Make something out of a problem. So in alignment with this insight we created a scene during the *Not Your Mama's Bus Tour,* where the audience was told that by the next stop a homeless woman would appear on the bus to tell a story or . . . she wouldn't show up. Whether this woman would appear in time or would be too late (or not show up at all) became part of the theater performance. How did this work out? Just wonderful! If she was there, the audience gave her a round of applause. If she wasn't there, the audience witnessed how incredibly difficult life on the streets can be.

Back to the scenarios that a good improv actor relishes: they are opposite to what we want in life. We do not want to have problems and "make something out of them"! We want happiness! Joy! Health! We want our lives to run smoothly.

Unfortunately this is not how life is. For anybody. All our lives are full of disappointments, setbacks, disasters, or, to sum it up, problems. What is our tendency when we are confronted with problems? To solve them, of course. Problems are nasty things. We want to get rid of problems, or to prevent them from ever happening in the first place. To be clear, there's nothing wrong with solving problems. But often, even if we can solve a problem, there is a missed opportunity. Now and then we can—like improv actors learn to do—make something out of a problem. Flip it into an opportunity. Make a non-appearance on a bus a memorable part of a show.

Flip thinking isn't easy. It requires a lot of skills. But don't be afraid. All these skills can be learned. Perhaps the hardest thing to develop, though, is a fundamental attitude to accept, like an improv actor, the things in life you can't change and then try to figure out what you can do with them. As long as you refuse to accept this fundamental attitude to life, flip thinking will be an illusion. But once you do accept this attitude, flip thinking becomes a skill to be mastered. So let's start now.

During the Dutch TV show *Great! De Leeuw Again,* hosted by comedian Paul de Leeuw and broadcast live, a streaker comes running into the studio, chanting "Stop animal cruelty," which is also written across his chest. Right at that moment, host De Leeuw is in the middle of a segment, a surprise phone call to a woman in her home, and he's just started chatting with her. Does he panic and cut to the commercials? No. He interrupts his discussion and calls to the streaker, "Wait there, I'll be right with you, then you'll get all the time you need." He then takes his time finishing the call. The streaker stands by onstage, looking somewhat bewildered but waiting politely for his turn. When De Leeuw finishes the call, he brings the streaker over to a chair onstage. "So, tell me what this animal cruelty's all about," he says.

A streaker during a live broadcast would usually be considered a problem. But by saying yes-and to the situation, Paul de Leeuw was able skillfully to transform it. Something that was at first an interruption to the program was flipped effortlessly into part of the program.

The incident exemplifies flip thinking. By approaching a problem as an opportunity, we are able to use it to our advantage. Flip thinking is a sort of psychological jujitsu. Just as you can learn to use your opponent's power to your advantage in a fight, you can use the power of a problem in your favor. Rather than doing battle with the problem, you allow the problem to do battle with itself.

Here's a second example. A young couple has just gotten married. The husband had lived with his parents until he was 31, and now the couple has moved into a house more than 93 miles from them. The parents come to visit every two weeks, armed with buckets, mops, and dusters, to clean the couple's house thoroughly, unasked. Obviously, the newlyweds aren't happy about this. They begin tidying their house before the parents' next visit, but the parents always seem to find some reason to complain about it being a pigsty and commence with their cleaning.

In desperation, the couple asks psychologist Paul Watzlawick for help. Known as being unconventional, Watzlawick gives them surprising advice, telling them not to clean up before the parents' next visit. In fact, the messier the place is, the better. If the parents start cleaning, he says, the young couple should act as if the cleaning is the most normal thing in the world, as though of course parents should work like crazy for their children, not lifting a finger to help. So that's what the couple do.

The next time the parents come to visit, the house is a complete disaster, strewn with piles of unopened bills and dirty clothes and mess everywhere. The parents work flat out for the whole weekend to get the house in order, and when they head for home on Sunday evening, they're so anxious to get away they leave skid marks in the drive. "They must think we're crazy!" the father says. "Yeah," his wife responds. "That's the last time we go to help them. They can just sort it out for themselves!"

Paul de Leeuw's response and the young couple's approach are counterintuitive. To come up with such a seemingly illogical response to a problem would seem to require a great deal of creativity. But actually, we can follow a number of logical steps.

For starters: in both cases, in one way or another the problem is completely ignored. Both the newlyweds and Paul de Leeuw seem to be refusing to react, as if there's really no problem at all. They even seem to be *enjoying* the situation. In most cases, if something happens that we don't want to be happening, we react with resistance—in the yes-but fashion. We try to get rid of the problem, or at the very least minimize it.

A streaker who runs screaming on to the set of a live broadcast?

Yes, but that can't happen. Stop him! Get him out of here!

Parents who invade to clean their children's home every fortnight?

Yes, but you just don't do that. Talk to them! Sort it out.

Of course, sometimes combatting a problem works, but often the result is akin to stomping on a snake under a carpet. The problem wriggles away, only to appear again. Quite a few problems are simply too complex to be solved by a straightforward, logical approach. As the saying goes, "Given the defini-tion of a problem, a problem is by definition unsolvable."

What's more, with yes-but thinking, we impose an uncon-structive limitation on a situation. We become fixated on how things "should be." The young couple wants the parents to con-form to a model of "good parents." De Leeuw would probably have preferred that his show went according to script. In such instances, we generally want to *repair* the situation. Our expec-tations lead us to perceive the situation as a problem. But the problem is not so much in reality as in our heads, and our yes-but thinking, according to our preconceptions of how the world "should be," perpetuates, or even contributes to, the problem. The trick is to learn to think outside the boundaries of your own limitations.

Ask yourself, who makes the rules of what defines being good parents, or how a live broadcast should unfold? Are there hard and fast laws? Flip thinking starts with letting go of the idea of what "should be" and being open to what "could be."

Step one: deconstruction— turn a problem into a fact

The first step in flip thinking is to move your mentality from "yes-but" to "yes." Literally say "yes" to the situation that pre-sents itself. Parents interfering isn't a problem to be resolved, it's a given. A fact. And let's face it, that's only sensible, because you can say what you like about reality, but by definition, it is what is. Accepting it saves a lot of hassle.

This first step (from problem to fact) is what I call the decon-struction. You pare a problem down to facts, removing all of the should-be and keeping what-there-is. In the course of this book, you will see that this process can sometimes be quite difficult. It's a bit like using a nutcracker to crack a hard nut, with the thickness of the shell equal to the firmness with which you hold on to your own fixed views about how reality should be.

Step two: reconstruction—
turn a fact into an opportunity

Next comes the paradoxical and creative perception of possibility. If parents want to do housekeeping, fine, let them help. Parents aren't *meant* to interfere; good parenting and such meddling are like oil and water. But our thinking has the incredible capacity to turn apparent contradictions into unexpected opportunities. In this second step, from yes to yes-and, you *pick up the pieces,* sweeping up the fragments of bare facts and figuring out what you can do with them. This transformation of fact into opportunity is the *reconstruction* phase, from what-is to what-could-be.

Flip thinking is sometimes complicated, painful, and time-consuming. It can involve grief, sadness, and resistance. In many cases, we need patience, tenacity, and confidence in order to achieve the flip. But sometimes the process can be surprisingly easy; more like a bubble bursting than a hard nut cracking. You get that "huh" feeling, a strange blend of "Really? Is it that simple?" and "Duh! I can't believe I didn't see that ages ago!"

Flip thinking doesn't follow a mathematical formula; it's more of an art, a skill. I really want to emphasize that. Quite a few people—in my experience, at least—expect flip thinking to be like a process of logical analysis, a type of science, which offers a new set of principles that they can apply to their problems with mathematical certainty. When it becomes clear that flip thinking doesn't work like that, they're disappointed. So, let me emphasize: flip thinking is not comprised of simple formulas; it is a creative process that adapts to circumstances.

To illustrate, consider a six-second clip that became wildly popular on YouTube. A father in Spain wanted to go for a walk to the supermarket with his three-year-old son. But the son wanted to go by car. They repeatedly exchanged just two words. The father stood on the path and kept saying "Walk," and the son, with his hand on the car door, replied "Here" each time. This was repeated one, two, three, four times. "Walk," "Here," "Walk," "Here." Then suddenly the father switched roles, and without skipping a beat, he said "Here." The surprising effect? His son immediately responded, "Walk," let go of the car door, and joined his father on the path. End of conflict.

The father utilized the flip-thinking strategy of role chang-ing, which worked perfectly on his three-year-old boy because three-year-olds want to be *autonomous,* to make their own deci-sions. If you say, "You're not allowed to clear your plate, or you'll grow up to be a big boy," they will clear their plates just to be contrary. To do what *they* want to do. But this strategy won't likely work for long with the boy. In a couple of months, he'll see through his father's trick, and if his father were to say "Here," he'd reply "Here."

Flip thinking doesn't provide failsafe, universal rules. It must adjust to circumstances, evolve. What it does provide is a way to continually expand your problem-solving repertoire.

Can you get good at flip thinking just by reading about it? Unfortunately not. You can only master it by doing it. It's like playing the piano in that sense—becoming accomplished takes years of practice. If you just read this book and don't actually try the techniques, it won't amount to anything more to you than a collection of entertaining stories. It's only by applying flip thinking to your own life that its power will become real for you.

Pianists have to work on their technique constantly, and flip thinking requires developing technique too. It involves multiple tools, and the trick is to apply the best ones for each situation. To emphasize the range of approaches, I like to refer to flip-thinking *strategy*. The term "strategy" is derived from warfare, in which sometimes the most effective approach is to attack, while at others it's to defend, and at still others, to wait and confer or negotiate. Warfare requires strategic insight, and so too does flip thinking involve a number of different strategies. I'll introduce you to 15 flip-thinking strategies over the course of this book. Some of them are concerned with the deconstruction phase; ways to strip back, dismantle, or unravel a problem. Others apply to the reconstruction phase, offering options for creating new opportunities.

Think of reading this book as like going on a flip-thinking journey. When you travel, you pack all the luggage you think you'll need for the journey. A certain amount of luggage is essential for the flip-thinking journey too; a number of *basic insights*. For that reason, the book consists of two main parts. The first introduces the luggage, the basic insights that will help you understand and get the most out of the strategies, and the second takes you on the journey itself, describing the 15 flip-thinking strategies. The third part is a helpful summary of the strategies.

Let's get started with Part 1.

The luggage.

flip thinking

Flip thinking (flip thought, Yes-and)

Thinking technique for transforming problems into opportunities; syn. yes-and thinking; cf. ant. yes-but thinking, thinking in terms of threats, dragons in your path

Using bold flip thinking, the board of directors was able to allay the press's suspicions; the psychiatrist advised the couple to flip-think their relationship patterns; once the negotiation adversaries had flip-thought the stalled talks, it was as if they had never been in conflict.

PART 1

The Luggage

Acceptance

If there is no solution to the problem then don't waste time
worrying about it. If there is a solution to the problem
then don't waste time worrying about it.

A young captain was in command of an impressive warship for the first time. One night the sea was churning, and the ship was shrouded in heavy fog. The captain received a signal from the bridge: a strange light was approaching directly, at high speed. The fearless captain didn't have to think for more than a second; he gave the order to transmit a message. "You're on a collision course. Change your course 20 degrees to the south immediately." The reply made the captain furious. He was given a counter-order. "Change your course 20 degrees to the north immediately." A few messages went back and forth in this fashion, with the captain demanding that the other party change its course, and the counter-command coming back the same every time. Finally, in desperation, the captain signaled: "I warn you, this is a battleship, we will shoot you." The answer was quick: "I warn you, this is a lighthouse!"[1]

One of the foundational insights of flip thinking is that there are some situations and problems that you simply have to accept. That's what this chapter's about. You might find this the odd chapter out in the book; after all, isn't flip thinking about change? Why would we spend time on things that we *can't* influence? Unfortunately, in practice we invest a great deal of energy in trying to change things that can't be changed. Like Don Quixote, we often try to make reality suit our wishes. And as long as we try to do that, as long as we focus our efforts on changing the unchangeable, we leave the things that we actually *could* change just as they are. Therefore, paradoxically, resistance often maintains the status quo, while acceptance itself can lead to change. In the words of provocative psychologist Jeffrey Wijnberg, "Acceptance is the highest form of change."

So, let's start at the beginning: acceptance. What's the first thing you think of when it comes to things that you can't change? Maybe the weather. When it's raining, there's nothing you can do to stop it. Or perhaps death. It's inevitable. We just have to accept it. We're all born and we all die. It's as simple as that. What about our moods? Can we change them? Can we say to ourselves "be happy" and just make ourselves happy? The answer is obviously yes and no. We can consciously influence our moods, but not completely control them. What about a relationship, or a company's culture? How do we know what we can change and what we can't?

As first laid out by the psychotherapist David Richo in his book *The Five Things We Cannot Change,* when we consider the world around us (including ourselves), five aspects of life are unchangeable.[2] To persist in trying to change these features of reality is a waste of effort, like a dog running up and down a beach barking at the waves.

1. Things change, and come to an end

Kicking in open door number one (and it's completely true): whatever you experience, it will at some time cease to exist. This includes everything that's precious to us; our relationships, our partners and children, our extended families, our work, our health, everything changes and comes to an end. A fact that is difficult to accept. The tragedy is that resistance is futile, but nonetheless we so desperately want to hold on to these things. Clinging to what once was is understandable, but the fact is that we have no other option than to let go. What's past is past and will never return. In the words of Eckhart Tolle, author of *The Power of Now*, "Nothing has happened in the past; it happened in the Now."

Incidentally, this observation also applies to the future. As Eckhart Tolle again pointed out, nothing happens in the future either. All happenings happen "in the Now." Flip thinking begins with the acceptance of the constant changeability of the here and now. Believing that we can prevent change, and loss, is building an illusion founded on quicksand.

Is that a hopeless conclusion? Perhaps it is, at first glance. But when you take a second look, you can see that it is actually an extremely positive observation. The continually changing "here and now" offers a never-ending source of inspiration. We can only unlock this inspiration when we let go of the illusion of control. Accepting the impermanence of life is not limiting; it is liberating.

2. Things don't always go according to plan

Another annoying truth we've all run up against. Maybe you've rented a great vacation house, but it turned out to be double-booked. Or your room looked out on a courtyard instead of the sea. And you've spent a year saving up for this vacation. Grrrr . . .

We tend to buy into an illusion of control over our lives, in part because this illusion is often supported. You flip a switch, and a light turns on. You order something online, and it's delivered on time. Quite a few things in life work in this almost miraculous way—according to plan, as I experienced as a child. My father was a market trader. Every day he had a cup of coffee in a café, and one day the bill he received was unusually high. In addition to his coffee, he was charged for six lemonades. He didn't drink lemonade, but I loved it, and I was with him that day. How had I managed to order six glasses without asking him for them? I had noted that to order coffee, my father put his hand up and waved his finger as if writing on his tab, saying his name, "Gunster." I had gone to sit at another table while my father was absorbed in reading his paper, and in exactly the same way I gestured, called out "lemonade" and "Gunster" and lo and behold, I was brought a glass of lemonade six times. My world was running according to plan. For this one time.

We get married, make sacred vows, and then get divorced. Not according to plan. We have children, hope that they are happy and healthy, bring them up properly, but then we get into an argument with them, and we become estranged. Not how we planned it. We start a business, but it goes bankrupt. An infinite number of pursuits in life don't go according to plan. And here, too, letting go is the key. Letting go of the idea that things will go according to plan, that our lives should be so manageable. "You just have to want it enough." "You've got to toughen up and persevere." We try to lift each other's spirits this way, and sometimes this advice is good. But often, it's not. Sometimes it's best not to persevere, but to let go.

Especially when it comes to intimate relationships, we tend to hold firm to notions of how the other person "should be" and we try to change our partners. Psychologist John Gottman, a leading specialist on relationships, found that as much as a shocking 69 percent of the conflicts in relationships are over things that can't be changed. One key to a successful marriage, he writes, is that both partners realize that there are quite a few things they can't change about the other. They have decided to accept each other "with all their faults."[3]

3. Life is not always fair

Yep, this is a tough one. Nothing's fair. Why were you laid off and not your colleague? Why do you feel unattractive and not that smart, while your sister is intelligent, incredibly attractive, and also has an irritatingly (to you) cheerful personality? How is it that someone who smokes lives to almost 100 while his neighbor, who always lived a healthy lifestyle, went to the gym three times a week and ate his vegetables, came down with an unknown virus while on vacation and passed away at the age of 36? That's hardly fair. Yet a fight against the unfairness of life is often a losing battle.

The pursuit of justice is noble; there's nothing wrong with that. As long as it's actually possible to have an impact. And that's precisely where the problem lies. If we're unable to exert an influence on our environment, then the belief in a just world quickly becomes a hindrance. An obstacle. In fact, this "just-world hypothesis" is such an obstructive belief that the social psychologist Melvin Lerner considers it one of our most significant attribution errors. We tend to believe—more or less consciously—that "what goes around comes around." "People get what they deserve." Given that most of us believe ourselves to be reasonable, civilized, and capable, we think we should be less likely to meet with misfortune. The idea that we may just have bad luck is deeply disturbing. We prefer to maintain the illusion that we hold our fate in our hands.

This is part of the appeal of fairy tales. The good guys always win. Justice prevails. Little Red Riding Hood beats the Big Bad

Wolf, Snow White is kissed awake (at least in the Disney version), and Hansel and Gretel escape from the wicked witch. Our religions, too, offer stories that help maintain the illusion of fairness. If you do the right thing, you'll go to heaven. Your good acts will be rewarded for eternity.

But fate can torment us. Suddenly. Cruelly. Viciously. Unpredictably. The Dutch writer Harry Mulisch used imagery of a swarm of mosquitoes to describe the randomness of life. We humans are like mosquitoes flying around in a group, with not a care in the world, when suddenly a bird flies through the swarm and snaps up mosquitoes left and right. How is that fair?!

4. Pain is part of life

Yes, the five things we must accept are getting more and more intense. Flip thinking regarding pain is particularly difficult. Why? Well, because, by definition, pain feels like a problem, not an opportunity.

We do everything we can to avoid pain. When that doesn't work, we try to get rid of it as quickly as possible, often involving denial. Your relationship ended? Don't dwell on it. Move on. Feeling burned out at work? You'll get past it! Just grit your teeth and deal with it. Grief over the death of a family member? Be strong. You can't let this beat you. Keep your chin up.

But pain is also a signal, a warning, as when a child feels pain if touching a hot stove. That pain protects him. Pain helps you avoid danger. When you're working out at the gym, it forces you to listen to your body, warning you not to overdo it. Trying to suppress pain, to push it away, is therefore not only pointless but counterproductive. Pain is an intrinsic part of life, and instead of denying it or fighting it, we are better off investigating whether we can use it to our advantage. Flip thinking helps with this.

Pain can provide insight, assist in making better decisions, and lead to personal transformation.

Research by the psychologist Gijs Jansen found that people who had experienced a good deal of misfortune in their lives often said that they led happier lives than those who had experienced less misfortune. "Upon inquiry it turned out that people with a lot of misfortune were better-trained in carrying on," Jansen explains.

> People who hadn't experienced much misfortune were much faster to throw in the towel. Those who had experienced failure regain hope and control over their lives, it's a matter of "learned optimism." People who are skilled at dealing with adversity have undoubtedly done this successfully in the past.[4]

Certainly, sometimes it seems like pain has no higher purpose to serve. The loss of a life partner or child are perhaps the most distressing examples of this. What could possibly be good, useful, or "transformative" about such events? They are simply devastating. Again, acceptance helps; accepting this truth that they are simply devastating; that's it, full stop. This pain, too, is an unavoidable part of life.

5. People are not always loving and loyal

This might be the hardest of the five to accept. There's always a risk that people will be disloyal to us. That they will say one thing and do another. With some people, we're not surprised, but what if it's your nearest and dearest? What if at your husband's funeral a strange woman shows up, half-hidden behind a tree, with a hanky, sniffling away? That might sound contrived, but these things happen. What if they happen to you?

We waste an enormous amount of energy trying to change these five big unchangeables.

"My husband snores."

OK, use earplugs. Sleep in another room. Snore back! Be happy, instead of angry, because as long as he's snoring, he's breathing.

"My father never paid me compliments."

OK. That's terrible. And it hurt. But it's in the past. You've made it in life just fine. You're a big boy of 63 now.

"My employees don't respect me."

And you still have employees? With that type of attitude? That's amazing! How do you pull that off?

"People are talking really loudly on their cellphones."

Well, at least you don't have to hear the other side of the conversation too!

"I'm getting old."

Aren't we all!

Complaining about things that you can't change is understandable, but before long, it turns into whining. Acceptance, by contrast, brings peace of mind.

The only thing is—and there's a big misunderstanding here—accepting reality is not the same as resigning yourself to it. Acceptance can sometimes lead to a different sort of change than you've been pressing for. Imagine you have a partner with a drinking problem. You've tried everything you can think of to get him to stop drinking. Finally, you realize you just have to accept the reality: "He has a drinking problem, and he may always drink." At that point you have two options: either to stay with him and accept the pain that goes with that, or decide to pack your bags and leave him.*

The irony is that the hope of change often holds off change, while the acceptance of unchangeability can usher in change.

This is the moment when I hope the penny will drop. One of the key insights of this book is that it's often our hope of change, our good intentions and well-meaning "solutions" that cause our problems to persist or, as you will see over the course of this book, to get even worse. Often problems will only disappear if we stop trying to solve them. Acceptance is the foundation of flip thinking.

The challenge is to learn to tell the difference between what we can and can't influence. The American theologian Reinhold Niebuhr sagely wrote in what's become known as "The Serenity Prayer," "God, grant me the serenity to accept the things I cannot change, the courage to change the things I can, and the wisdom to know the difference." Was that a new insight? Not at all. The Stoic philosopher Epictetus offered the same essential advice, less poetically, in the first century AD: "Happiness and freedom begin with a clear understanding of one principle: some things are within our control, and some things are not. It is only after you have faced up to this fundamental rule and learned to distinguish between what you can and can't control that inner tranquility and outer effectiveness become possible." Only when we stop clinging compulsively to what "should be," and then look at what is really there, can we open ourselves to

---

* Of course I don't mean to say that accepting his drinking should automatically lead to leaving him. Acceptance might also mean accepting the pain of continuing to try to help him quit. There are many ways of accepting.

what could be. From problem to fact, from fact to opportunity. From yes-but to yes, from yes to yes-and.

Byron Katie is a remarkable woman who one day came to the shocking realization that she was constantly resisting reality and saw how much energy it had cost her, and how unhappy it made her. After reaching that insight, she went on to write a number of incredibly popular books on self-inquiry that positively influenced thousands of people's lives. She summed up the problem with resisting reality:

> People often referred to me as the woman who made friends with the wind. Barstow is a desert town where the wind blows a lot of the time, and everyone hated it; people even moved from there because they couldn't stand the wind. The reason I made friends with the wind— with reality—is that I discovered I didn't have a choice. I realized that it's insane to oppose it. When I argue with reality, I lose—but only 100 percent of the time. How do I know that the wind should blow? It's blowing![5]

Last, a bonus.

You can't change reality. The thing you *can* change is what you do with reality. As the saying goes, "It's not the cards you're dealt, but how you play the hand." Here's one of my favorite anecdotes to illustrate this point, about a man whose criminal history began when he was an adolescent. He progressed from theft, to drug dealing, to armed robbery, spending more time in prison than out of it. Now, this man had two sons, and despite being raised by the same parents, they were as different as night and day. One son was a copy of his father: he led a life of crime, was convicted numerous times, and spent a great deal of time in prison. The other son led a totally different life: he married and had two children, holding down a respectable, almost boring, job and had no criminal record. Researchers interested in the nature/nurture debate, about how much our behavior is influenced by our genes and how much is accounted for by upbringing, asked the two sons independently, "How would you explain the life you lead?" To which both, again independently, replied, "What do you expect, with a father like that?"

Observation

On the limitations of our perception

Where judgment begins, observation ends.

In the 1970s, at a seminary in Princeton, two social psychologists named John Darley and Daniel Batson conducted an experiment that was both amusing and poignant. A selection of male students at the seminary were asked to give a talk on the biblical story of the Good Samaritan. If you're not familiar with it (though I'd be surprised), it's a story about a benevolent Samaritan, from an ethno-religious group in the Middle East, who helps a man who has been beaten and left for dead by the side of the road. The students had to walk to a lecture theater in another building to give their talks, and what they didn't know was that, on their way, they would pass a person collapsed on the ground, theatrically moaning and groaning in apparent pain. Did the students act as Good Samaritans? Most did not. Only 40 percent of them stopped and asked if everything was okay. The other 60 percent rushed past, and some of them were even so focused on getting to their talk that they actually stepped over the fellow in need.[1]

Accepting reality as it is, is a virtue. But do we see reality as it is? A farmer and a scientist are sitting in a car. The farmer looks outside.

"Look," he says, "the sheep have been shorn."

"Completely?" the scientist asks. "Are you sure?"

"Yes," the farmer replies, "use your eyes!"

The scientist says, "I wouldn't dare to be so confident about it. I would say, the side that we can see has been shorn; whether the other side has been shorn too remains to be seen."

To be able to flip-think, we need to deconstruct problems into facts, but observing the facts can be harder than you'd think. We often don't take in what our eyes observe. Instead, we see what we *think* we see. Let's do a little test to investigate this. A cleaner was cleaning the windows on the 61st floor of a skyscraper in the heart of New York City. While washing the windows, he fell. He wasn't wearing a safety harness, and there was nothing else to break his fall. Yet he wasn't hurt. How could this be? Have a think about it, I'll give the answer a little later . . .

It's essential that you know what you want out of life; what you're moving toward. But knowing where you are is sometimes even more important. Being able to observe reality, the facts of the here and now, is vital. A group of managers at an IT company I worked with learned this in an intriguing way while doing a survival course in the Ardennes, Belgium. They were given a detailed map of the area, driven to the middle of the forest in a car with blacked-out windows, and told they would have to make their way out. They couldn't wait—with gorgeous weather, a great team, plenty of provisions, the exercise would be a pleasure. But once they'd stepped out of the car their enthusiasm turned to uncertainty. Why? Did they not know where they had to go? No, that wasn't the problem, they had the map. The problem was that they didn't know where they were.

Seeing reality as it is, knowing the facts, is an absolute prerequisite for flip thinking. But observing reality is easier said than done. This is true not only for people, but for every other type of organism too. If you put a frog in a jar with live flies he'll be fine because he'll eat them. But if you put dead flies in the jar, he won't eat them and will eventually die. Frogs notice movement, but not stationary objects.

What's true of frogs is true for people in our own ways; our powers of observation are limited. Consider our senses. We can only perceive sounds with a frequency of between 20 and 20,000 Hz. Anything else we simply don't hear. As for light, again, we see only a limited number of wavelengths. We can't see the shorter wavelengths of ultraviolet light that bees, for example, can, and as for longer wavelengths, our sight stops at the infrared part of the spectrum. Snakes can still see fairly well in this range, but as the waves continue to grow longer they also lose sight.

Our perceptions are also influenced by what we don't know. In their book *Systems Thinking,* Jaap Schaveling, Bill Bryan, and Michael Goodman describe research conducted by a team at the start of the last century. The team asked someone from a small town in South America to spend a morning walking around New York City. In the afternoon they met with him to discuss what he had observed. He told them that when he went to the port he had been impressed by someone who "could carry three combs of bananas" (these are not the small bunches that we buy in the shops, but the enormous ones that hang from the tree). In his village, most people could carry only one comb, and the really strong people could manage two on a good day, but three . . . that was unheard of. On further investigation, the astounded team discovered that the porters at the harbor used handcarts. They surmised that because the man wasn't familiar with such carts, he hadn't made note of it.[2]

Another way in which our brains limit our observations is

tunnel vision. When we're concentrating on one thing, we don't observe other things. Cats do this too. The easiest way to approach a cat is when he's deep in concentration, on the point of pouncing on a mouse. This effect was dramatically illustrated in a famous study conducted at Harvard University. The subjects were asked to watch a video that showed two teams of three people passing basketballs to one another; one team wearing white T-shirts and the other black T-shirts. The subjects were asked to count how many times the ball was passed in the air and how often it was passed on the ground. Halfway through the film, an actor in a gorilla suit leisurely walked right through the group of people passing the balls, performed an elegant twirl, and then walked out of the other side of the frame. After viewing the video, the subjects were asked if they had noticed anything unusual. The majority answered, "Nothing." Even when asked, "Did you see a black gorilla?" almost 50 percent said no. When the subjects were shown the video a second time, they could hardly believe it was the same film.[3]

We unconsciously narrow our attention in regular life too. Give new parents a hotel room next to a railway station with plenty of creaking and rattling of trains, and after a short time, they'll have no trouble sleeping through it. But if their baby makes even a peep, despite all that noise, they'll instantly pick up on it.

I was once at a flea market in Utrecht looking for a Rubik's Cube, wondering if anyone would still sell them. To my total amazement it seemed as if every stall had one on offer. It was like the whole country wanted to get rid of their cubes that morning. But, if I hadn't set out to look for one, I probably wouldn't have seen any of them.

Awareness of the brain's tendency to focus on relevant information and—therefore—simultaneously to shut out irrelevant

or conflicting information is extremely important to flip thinking. The more narrowly you focus, the fewer possibilities and
opportunities you'll be alert to.

The list of "sloppy observations" is endless, and the consequences are often problematic. In his book *Why I'm Always
Right,* Eric Rassin, a specialist in legal psychology, describes that
the tendency for people to see only what they think is there
explains several high-profile mistakes made in criminal investi-
gations. Once investigators have come up with a theory for a
crime, they take less notice of facts that contradict this theory.

The following task allows you to experience tunnel vision in
action. Let's say that a researcher presents you with a set of three
numbers—2, 4, and 6. The researcher gives you the following
instructions: "These three numbers follow a certain rule, a certain pattern. Your task is to identify this rule. You can give me
sets of three numbers as many times as you like. I'll tell you each
time whether they're right or not, until you've figured out the
rule."

Have a think about the task.

Which set of numbers would you give to the researcher?

This little test was used in a classic experiment by Peter Watson of the University of London. Watson discovered that most
students assumed that the rule was n, n+2, n+4, or "add two to
the previous number." When students tested this theory, for example by giving the set 3-5-7 or 10-12-14, Watson answered,
"Correct." The students' assumption was confirmed and they
answered that the rule was "add two every time." To this Watson
replied, "Wrong." Another rule was operating. The students
would then develop a new theory and propose a new rule to
Watson. For example, "The middle number is exactly halfway
between the two other numbers." If they tested this with sets of
numbers like 13-16-19 or 10-15-20, it once again seemed to be

correct. But this theory turned out to be wrong too. What happened next? The students' formulas became increasingly complex. What was happening? The formula was actually very simple: every second number is greater than the first, every third number is greater than the second. So 1-2-1412 would also have received the response, "Correct." However, the students rarely tried such "illogical" sets of numbers. If they had, they would have come up with the answer much more quickly. So why didn't they give those types of sets? Because their assumption about what the rule *should* be impeded the view of what the rule *could* be.[4]

A bottle is lying on its side, with a number of bees in it. A light, switched on, hangs above the bottle. There's no lid on the bottle; it's open. What will the bees do to get out of the bottle? Bees understand that where there's light, there must be a way out—so they fly toward the light in the glass, and they keep doing this until they end up lying at the bottom of the bottle, exhausted. Flies, by contrast, don't have the knowledge about light indicating an exit. If you put them into the same bottle they will fly around madly. The result? They will (eventually) find the way out.

What's true of the bees is true of us, too. Having information can be a handicap in creative thinking. The more we think we know about how to solve a problem, the greater the risk we'll get stuck in a rut. Take the mystery I gave you at the start of this chapter, in which the cleaner is washing the windows on the 61st floor, falls, and yet doesn't get hurt. What's the explanation? He's cleaning the inside of the windows.

We use information from our experiences to construct theories that can blind us to the reality of new situations. And we often cling to these theories, rather than opening our minds up to valuable bits and pieces of information that don't fit neatly into them. We're overly fond of great hypotheses and logical arguments, which seem to offer clear explanations. But even the most logical theory may not be correct. The facts of any situation are often more reliable sources of explanation than any theory. An example: a Dutch education committee paid a visit to an experimental school in Canada, which used the principles of natural learning, first established in 1968 when the Sudbury Valley School was founded in the US. Its core philosophy was for teachers to follow the natural curiosity and development of children. Everybody in the school, teachers, children, and staff, was responsible for his or her own choices, learning, and future, and all were treated as equal citizens. The school in Canada adopted these principles. The approach worked fabulously; the school boasted enthusiastic students, a committed team of teachers, and satisfied parents. But one of the visiting Dutch educators wasn't happy. More than that—he found the visit depressing. A fellow teacher on the trip asked him why, and he responded, "This school, it's a nice experiment, but I don't understand why everyone's walking around so jubilantly, it can't be *that* good. There's not a single educational theory to back up what they're doing here."

Which theories are you clinging on to? And how much proof do you have to back them up? Let's consider a set of common assumptions that are viewed by many instead as expressions of fact.

"You have to keep your promises."

That sounds logical, but should you always really? Even if you've promised something stupid? Or made a promise that you can't keep? Or if you've changed your mind?! What if others are taking advantage of you because of a promise?

"You have to get a college degree if you want to have a meaningful career and contribute to society."

Oh? Are there no careers that don't require a degree? Do you even have to have a *career*? What exactly *is* a career, anyway?! Isn't being a hairdresser having a career and contributing to society? Or being a builder? What about being a mother?

"Couples are best off having a monogamous relationship."

Interesting. Is that so? Always, for everyone? How does that square with the fact that one in three marriages fail?! If you can love more than one person one after the other, then why not at the same time? After all, you can love your mother *and* your father?

"In this life, it's important to mean something to other people."

Hmm. Are we here then, by definition, for other people? Is that essential, or an option? When do you "mean" something exactly? Is that always clear?

"You have to make the most of your talents."

All talents? Who says? Why? To what purpose? What if you don't have much in the way of talent?

"Sex between cousins is irresponsible."

Oh yeah? Why? Because of the risk of children with birth defects? But what if they use contraceptives responsibly and both are above the age of consent? Is there still a reason against it? To take the scenario a step further—what if they fall in love with each other in their old age and children are no longer a possibility? Is it still wrong?

You might be angered by these questions, or feel indignant. I can understand that. But I'm not being provocative for no reason. I'm challenging whether you're prepared to look philosophically at your own assumptions about reality, or whether you are like the educator who believes that reality must be secondary to theory.

I'm giving you all these examples not to force you to change your opinion, but to challenge you to open your mind. To throw the shutters open and let a fresh spring wind blow through your head. Flip thinking starts with an open mind. Curiosity. Thinking in possibilities. Nothing's compulsory. Everything's allowed. If you decide that something's compulsory, that's fine, I do so myself, like everybody else does. We all have our values and principles. It would not only be naive but also impossible to live without them. Values and principles influence our behavior. But you are the one to decide what's compulsory and what's not. Nobody else. As long as you see the world through the lens of firmly entrenched theories, you will never be able to see facts as they actually are—let alone be able to deal with problems in a novel way.

Research in psychology has revealed many other ways that our perceptions are skewed. For example, there's the halo effect: the tendency to ascribe additional positive qualities to people who already possess certain "positive" qualities. We think that people who are beautiful will be smart too (even without having seen any sign of intelligence). This may explain in part why we are inclined to offer attractive people a job more readily than less attractive people. Sad, but true. It's a real handicap for those less attractive people among us.

Consider also the primacy effect: the tendency to attach far more importance to the first pieces of information we receive than to those that follow. I see this with my name, Berthold Gunster. Many people pronounce my last name as though it's German and has an umlaut, like Günther or Günter (more of an "ue" sound). Why? It's because of my first name, Berthold. That sounds German, so they assume I'm also German. How do I know this is why it happens? Because my oldest son, Jan, never has this problem. "Jan" is a common Dutch name, so people pronounce "Gunster" in the Dutch way, with no umlaut.

The primacy effect is important to consider when it comes to our opinions because we generally form them quickly. Counter-information we may receive thereafter is often not considered adequately. This is why it's important that for every opinion you form, you examine the manner in which you came to that conclusion. It's also good to ask yourself, "Would the opposite also be true?" And always keep in mind the difference between a fact and an opinion. Can rich people be noble-minded? Can parents be selfish? Might an accused criminal have had good intentions? Could white be black, and black white?

Another foible of our thinking is the "contrast effect." If you're quite smart but you're part of a group consisting entirely of highly intelligent people, they'll consider you to be of average (or below average) intelligence. But if you're part of a group of average thinkers, you could be seen as the Einstein of your gang. As the saying goes, in the land of the blind, the one-eyed man is king.

One more cognitive distortion that taints our thinking is the "similar-to-me effect": we unconsciously have an affinity for people we see as more like us. Conversely, we have more distrust of people we see as less like us. Then there's the "more exposure effect." The more often we've seen something, the more familiar it feels and therefore the more comfortable we feel around it. This explains the power of constantly repeating advertisements: the more often we see them, the more positive an association we make with a brand.

These examples of our cognitive biases and flawed ways of thinking are by no means complete. Psychologists have uncovered many more. I offer these few to drive home the point that seeing the facts as they truly are, and drawing conclusions that do not misrepresent reality, is a complex task. If you want to learn how to flip-think, you must learn to exercise a great deal of caution when it comes to thinking that you know the truth of any given situation. We get things wrong more often than we get them right.

Psychologist Daniel Kahneman has conducted extensive research into the flaws in human thinking, and he has revealed grave injustices to which it can lead. If there is one group of people you would hope could assess facts accurately, it would have to be judges. So what did Kahneman find? That defendants who were sentenced just after judges had eaten had a significantly higher chance of being acquitted than other defendants. Certainly one's fate should not be dependent on whether or not a judge has a full stomach.[5]

So, what does all this mean for flip thinking?

First, that we must constantly train ourselves to exercise a healthy dose of caution about our theories and observations, and search intensively for facts. As Goethe said, "The hardest thing to see is what is in front of your eyes."

Second, we must realize that our brains want to construct a complete picture. Our minds don't like disconnected bits of information; they want the bits to fit together into a clear story. Robert Fritz cautions in his book *The Path of Least Resistance*, "Don't fill in the gaps." The ability to consider incomplete and often seemingly contradictory information without fitting it into a reassuringly clear understanding—to accept what you don't know—is a basic skill required for flip thinking.

Third, we should accept that we will all, always, have blind spots. We don't see a full version of reality. We see chiefly what we're primed to see, or want to see. We're like the blindfolded people in the proverbial story of trying to identify an elephant. The one who feels the leg calls out, "It's a tree," the one who feels the tail says, "It's a feather duster," and the one at the trunk shouts, "It's a vacuum cleaner!" Before you assume that you know all the facts, always take a good look around to check that there aren't any more "fragments" available to help you see a situation differently. Get out of your head and challenge yourself to observe properly. The more of reality you can see, the more opportunities to flip-think you can discover.

Problems

On thinking in terms of problems

In reality there are no problems, only facts.

At this point it's a good idea to take a little philosophical detour to consider the word "problem." Given that flip thinking always starts with a problem, it's good to be sure we have a solid understanding of our raw material. What are we talking about, exactly, when we use the word "problem"?

The word suggests that a problem is a disruptive, scary, or irritating thing, like a bear in your living room. Bear gone, problem gone. Or the rain might be the problem, or a complaining child, or that disappointing vacation house looking on to the courtyard rather than the beautiful vista. But the reality is more complex. A problem is never just *one* thing; by definition, a problem consists of two things: (1) an idea or desire about how reality should be, and, (2) a perception of reality as being in conflict with that idea or desire. It seems as if the bear is the problem, but the actual problem consists of the tension between (1) the fact of the bear's presence, and (2) your desire to stay alive.

Perhaps that sounds absurd, and I admit it might be a bit of a stretch, but stay with me. As a thought experiment, imagine that your goal is to make a film of you being eaten by a bear (cool!). Then, of course, the bear would not be a problem. Whether you've got a problem due to its presence depends on your intention. The bear is merely a fact of the situation. Similarly, the weather, complaining children, or a courtyard-facing holiday house don't present problems in and of themselves. The way in which we define our expectations determines whether we will experience certain facts as constituting a problem—or not. The logical conclusion of this insight can only be that there cannot be problems in the world around us. Things are what they are. Without meaning. Until we attach meaning to them. Reality is just data that we interpret.

I do understand that in normal human life, an enormous bear in the living room is hugely problematic. But let's shift the perspective. Imagine you're the bear, and you're hungry.

I know this example is far-fetched, so let's consider an actual experience I had. When my oldest son was 11 years old, whenever I went for a shower, the shower head was too low. I'd seen a few times that he was the one who'd used the shower before me. Finally, one morning I had a word with him about the problem, asking, in irritation, that he put the shower head back where it was. He listened intently and then answered, "I'll do that, no problem. Now, is it okay if I mention something that annoys me every day?" I said sure, go ahead. "Every morning when I take a shower," he said, "the shower head is too high. Could you please put it back where it was in the future?"

What's a problem for one person can be the ideal for the other, and vice versa. This underscores that, objectively, there aren't any problems, only facts, and that we can either interpret facts as problems (because they cause us trouble); as facts (or "just the way things are" because we are neutral toward them); or as opportunities (because we see positive potential in them).

When it comes to problems, it's actually quite simple. There are only two types: when something's missing that we think should be there, or something's there that we think shouldn't be there. That's it.

A few years ago I organized a training program in eastern Europe as part of a partnership project. I posited the same thought to a room full of post-communist professors, entrepreneurs, and students: "In reality there are only facts. However large or complex the problem is," I said, "we can always deconstruct it down to a combination of facts and desires." A woman stood up and interrupted me in perfect English. "Sir, it's easy for you to say 'problems don't exist,' perhaps that's true in your country, but here you only have to leave the building and the problems are there for the taking. Two of my best friends, an elderly couple, live on the eleventh floor of an apartment building. The water pipes are broken and the lift only goes up to the fifth floor. If they need water, they first have to take two buckets to the fifth floor, then they take the lift down to the ground and get the water. Then they take the buckets of water to the fifth floor in the lift and after that they still have to carry them up the stairs to the eleventh floor. How can you say that there are no problems? Surely the problem with the water is a fact? And the lift doesn't work! How can you say that there aren't any problems?"

I thought, *OK, if this is how it's going to be, then we'll wrestle for a bit.* I started cautiously. "Let's start by observing that the broken water pipes are indeed a problem for these people. But what would plumbers think? For them, broken water pipes represent work. But let's take it even further. There are similar problems in the West too. Much smaller. I know. Incomparably smaller. But in essence the structure of a problem is the same. For example, I'm sitting quietly watching the World Cup football on my television, the Netherlands is playing, and ten minutes remain in the game. Suddenly I'm incredibly thirsty. So I have to get up, walk to the kitchen, fill a glass with water and then I walk back to the television. And sure enough, I've just missed a goal!"

The indignation in the room was rising.

Where was this story going?

"I'm exaggerating, of course, to make a point," I went on, "but essentially the same rules apply in Poland as in the Netherlands: first, you want a drink, then you have the problem of how to get it. That problem is for us very small and for you obviously a lot bigger, and I respect that, but on a structural level the same laws apply: the desire is the source of the problem. Not the water pipes. The water pipes are just a fact."

"But," she replied, "how do you mean *want* to drink, these people have to drink water, don't they? It's not a question of free choice."

"Who says they have to drink?" I asked.

"If you don't drink, you'll die."

"So," I asked, "what's wrong with that?"

There was a momentary pause.

Then she said, "But you have to live!"

"Do you have to live?" I asked. "Is that so? Who says? Why? Is there a sort of need for you to spend your life here, as a type of duty?"

Another pause. Then she replied, "No. But surely you want to live?!"

"Yes," I replied, "and that's where all the trouble starts. You want to live! You have ambitions, plans, desires. Sometimes they work out, great; sometimes they don't work out, you have a problem. You're cycling along, when suddenly you get a flat tire. Annoying. Problem. There is a very effective way not to experience that problem: just don't want to cycle. Or to go a step further: if only the bike had never been invented. Then we would never have had flat tires.

"In life there is constant tension between our desires and reality. That means that we will constantly experience problems. That's just how it works. You're young, you're in love, you'd really like to start a relationship, and you do. Hooray! But before you know it you have all kinds of relationship problems. There is a simple way to make sure you never have to deal with relationship problems: never start a relationship. There are two very simple laws: if you want to have as few problems as possible, you have to want as little as possible, and if you want a lot, then you will therefore experience a lot of problems. As long as we want to live, we will want things—and as long as we want things, we will create problems. That's okay. Desire is an inseparable part of life, of being human. But it *is* important to realize that our desires and needs cause us to experience some facts as problems. A lift is a lift. A pipe is a pipe. None of it means anything. It's only when we start a relationship with them, when we have desires and needs, that we give meaning to the world around us. Desire is at the source of every problem."

Some people think that in saying this, I mean that we can—or even should—experience reality as problem-free. If only we're detached enough. If only we don't desire anything. And of course that's not how life works; we constantly have desires and expectations. Sure, we can escape, travel the world and meditate on a rock, trying to be completely detached from earthly concerns and desire nothing. Perhaps we'll achieve the spiritual experience of being completely in the here and now, and totally free of problems. But as soon as you want something to drink or need to go to the toilet then you're hassled again. And the effort has already gone completely wrong if you feel that you *have* to have the spiritual experience of sitting on a rock without a care in the world. If you sit down because you feel you must have that experience, then you're sitting down with an expectation. And that works against it being fulfilled. You'll be constantly evaluating whether or not you're feeling carefree. Sigh.

I'm not ridiculing those of us who are seeking enlightenment. My point is that desires are an essential part of being human. Just as a tree "wants" to grow, so a child longs to dance in the rain, a young person to fall in love, and an adult to have a life partnership, to have a baby, or to excel at work. There's nothing wrong with that. We desire things. Wishes, needs, and ambitions make us who we are. They're our life source, the thing that keeps us going. But having desires necessarily involves the risk that a desire won't be fulfilled. Pain, grief, mourning, and disappointment are just as much a part of life as joy, happiness, ecstasy, or pleasure. But it's extremely important to realize that this is true only because of our hopes and expectations. This understanding is contrary to the typical way we think about how life works. Which is why we need to flip our thinking.

Life will often not conform to our desires and expectations. When we're in a traffic jam, we think the traffic is the problem; it's not. It's only a fact. The problem arises from our expectation that we will not encounter a jam. What's more, this flawed perspective prevents us from appreciating that *we* are also part of the traffic jam.

If we want to live our lives in a yes-and way, we must adopt this philosophical mindset. The reality around us contains only facts, and wherever in the world we're born, in whichever era and to whichever parents, we'll always have difficult experiences. Once we accept that life is simply not fair, we can shift our attention from "what isn't" and "should be" to "what is" and "could be." Or, as Sartre said, "Freedom is what you do with what's been done to you." What's been done to you can't be changed. What you can do with it is the theme of this book.

What if everything goes right?

On resistance to change

There are people who prefer to say "yes" and there are
people who prefer to say "no." Those who say "yes"
are rewarded by the adventures they have. Those who
say "no" are rewarded by the safety they attain.

—Keith Johnstone, pioneer of improvisational theater

The Israeli company Kapro had been making the same construction tools for years. During a workshop they wanted to
look at whether they could expand their range. One of the in-
struments Kapro made was a spirit level, which allows you to
determine whether or not a surface is level. The device has been
made in essentially the same form for hundreds of years: a bar
with a liquid-filled tube in the middle and a little bubble in the
liquid, which moves left to right as you tilt the level one way or
the other, and settles right in the middle when the device is
perfectly level.

To innovate a new version, the workshop participants used
the multiplication technique, which is very simple. You divide a
contraption into parts, lay them in a row, and consider how you

might build on what works about them, multiplying their effectiveness. The spirit level had only two components: the bar and the liquid-filled tube. What could they do? Multiply the number of bars? Or the number of tubes? Before long, to the astonishment of the participants, the task led to the "obvious" solution of adding more tubes, at various angles, to the level. After all, construction regularly involves features built at angles, such as sloped ceilings. If a spirit level only works horizontally, a builder has to fiddle with little bits of paper and blocks in order to measure an incline correctly. It's not only cumbersome but inaccurate. A level with tubes at different angles would allow for quick checks that angles are right. As a result of this innovation, a whole new generation of spirit levels went into production. Sales tripled in four years, and before long exports to America and Europe were booming. A simple method led to an innovation that had been waiting for hundreds of years to be conceived.[1]

The Kapro story is interesting for many reasons. First, of course, because the discovery was so simple yet so brilliant. Second, because the discovery led to an innovation that was immediately successful, while many innovations take time to find a good market. The third reason is the most intriguing—it's hard to believe that no one had thought of the change a long time ago! Why had builders worked with the classic spirit level for so long without asking themselves how it could be improved? This story highlights that, for the most part, people are averse to change. We generally only want to make a change if we *have* to. We really don't like change. Change is scary. It seems dangerous. If there's no other option, okay, we'll make a move. But what if everything's going all right? Why should we? The biggest threat to *great* is therefore *good*.

Let's say that I asked you, "Do you like change?" What's the first thing that comes to mind? For me, it's a counter-question. Well, what's going to change? Am I going to lose something? Or will I gain something? Until we know what kind of change we're talking about, we'll be wary. All change involves at least some anxiety. And if a change goes against our will and is without our agreement, we'll feel resentment, or anger, and will resist. What do you mean "change"? We'll decide that for ourselves.

What about positive change, which could lead to great success, say a higher level job at a new company? Often we're ambivalent. We've learned that success comes with a price tag. Take the case of earning great wealth. People listed in the *Fortune* 500 need to have serious home security systems because they're at high risk of being robbed. Then there's the high stress usually involved in the work they do, the long hours, the traveling . . .

Imagine that you win $16 million in the lottery. For the first few days you're obviously going to be thrilled. But what happens once the champagne glasses have been washed up and you've taken down the streamers and balloons? What are you going to do with all that money? Invest it? You've got to work out how. And will you quit your job? What if you really like what you do? But maybe, if you don't need the money anymore, you won't like the job so much. If you do quit your job, what will you do with your time? Research shows that winning a large lottery prize involves so much stress and hassle that winners are initially less happy.[2]

Both earning and winning a fortune are great, but with that success comes a whole lot of change, and that means a whole lot of uncertainty. And that's what most of us don't like. Take the Dutch; we love stability. The Netherlands is one of the most-insured countries in the world. In fact, until the 1960s, you used to be able to buy rain insurance from Dutch Railways. If you took a day trip by train, say to visit Amsterdam, and on the day of your journey it rained more than a certain amount designated by your insurance, you could get a refund for the ticket. Can you imagine? At the end of a rainy day the railway stations must have been packed with passengers clamoring for their money, perhaps actually feeling grateful for the heavy rain!*

So what's the result of the aversion to uncertainty? Let's follow the logic to its ironic conclusion. Here's a simple deduction. If success can actually lead to uncertainty, what leads to certainty? That's right, failure! This is why people so often breathe a sigh of relief when a big project fails. "You see," they'll say, "I knew it!" Now things can remain the same. As the saying goes, "Better the devil you know than the devil you don't." In our desire for stability, we think we're gaining safety. But it may be that the opposite is the case. Research into the causes of burnout, in which many variables were studied, such as age, place of work, sex, level of education, and type of work, shows that the best predictor is the number of years a person remains in the same job. In the words of the Brazilian writer Paulo Coelho, "If you think adventure is dangerous, try routine. It's lethal."

Clearly we are built for change, and challenge. You could say that intellectual change is healthy for the mind, just as exercise is healthy for the body. The reverse is also true: eliminating challenge and change from our lives is actually unhealthy.

Back to flip thinking.

What is the relationship between the pursuit of stability and flip thinking?

The answer is simple. Our built-in tendency to seek stability and security is at odds with the technique of flip thinking.

---

* The Netherlands also has one of the highest savings rates in the world. We absolutely love money in the bank. How can you make a Dutchman happy? With a 30-year fixed interest rate.

Those who challenge themselves to flip-think problems are striving for change, even if—as with the classic spirit level that worked well for its original purpose—that change isn't necessary. Flip thinking goes hand in hand with disruption. That's scary, but remember, being receptive to change can lead to a leap forward, maybe even one that's been long overdue.

Antifragility

On growth through resistance

To fly we have to have resistance.
—Maya Lin, designer and sculptor

In the 1960s, the Australian athlete Derek Clayton was one of the least-gifted marathon runners in the world. Standing almost six feet, and with a relatively low oxygen uptake, is a body type anything but ideal for long-distance running. But he compensated by working harder than anyone else, running more than 160 miles a week.

Although this strict regimen initially worked, at a certain point he hit a wall: he reached the apparent limit of his possibilities. With a personal best of 2 hours and 17 minutes, more than 5 minutes slower than the world record, he couldn't compete with the top runners of his generation. Past a certain point, working harder didn't result in improved performance. On the contrary: in 1967, while he was training for the Fukuoka marathon in Japan, it resulted in a serious injury.

Clayton was forced to take a month off to recover. After that month, devastated that he might not be able to make up for the ground he'd lost in training, he decided to run another marathon before the Fukuoka race to test the extent to which he had recovered. What happened? To his surprise (and that of the whole world), after a month without training, he beat his personal best by more than eight minutes. Clayton went on to become the first man in history to run a marathon in less than 2 hours and 10 minutes. His training wasn't his secret; *not* training was.

Since then, dozens of similar stories from the sporting world have been reported of a physical setback and recovery making the body stronger than ever. It's as if the recovery process overcompensates for the damage done.

Economist Nassim Nicholas Taleb came to international fame with his bestselling book *The Black Swan,* on highly improbable events that shape our lives, often in dramatic ways. He considers his subsequent book, *Antifragile,* to be his magnum opus, the crowning achievement of his philosophical oeuvre on uncertainty, risk, and human error. In the book, he examines the capacity to absorb harm and cope with disorder and unpredictability, and use those challenges to become stronger. Things that can do this, from individuals to cities, economies, political systems, bacterial colonies, and even cultural phenomena like rumors, are antifragile. They not only adapt and survive, they have the magical ability to use adversity as a means of advancing. He uses the metaphor of the multi-headed monster Hydra from Greek mythology to describe antifragility: every time one of its heads was hacked off, two grew in its place.

So what's the relationship between antifragility and flip thinking? Well, we could say that an organism, or a system, that rebounds from a setback to become stronger is flip thinking—seeing opportunity where it wouldn't be expected. The phenomenon of antifragility also teaches us a valuable strategy we can employ in flip thinking: sometimes, rather than actively trying to solve a problem, we should simply leave a situation be and allow antifragile capability to do the work. We don't have to intervene; in fact, we need to stop interfering. Flip thinking sometimes means stepping aside and leaving things to get on with the problem solving on their own.

When you do strength training, you deliberately damage your muscles. This is an example of good stress. Using heavy weights to put an excessive load on the muscular system causes small tears in your muscles. What is the result? The body doesn't just repair the tears; it creates even *more* muscle mass to compensate. Physiotherapists call this supercompensation. An important point is that the growth doesn't happen during training—only the damage occurs then. The growth happens during the rest periods between training sessions.

Another example of good stress is the distraction that motorists need in order to stay fresh and alert. Straight, uncrowded roads are monotonous and drivers let their attention lapse, or may even fall asleep. The slight stress of bends in the road, or cars suddenly changing lanes or merging into traffic from an on-ramp, keeps drivers on their toes. We looked at a similar effect earlier with work: the longer people keep doing the same job, the less challenging it is and the greater the chance of burnout. Adding a healthy dose of tension and instability in our work lives keeps us more engaged.

Another way antifragility shows up in our lives is in the phenomenon of post-traumatic growth. Much attention has been paid to post-traumatic stress, but psychologists are paying more and more attention to how people rebound from trauma. Two professors from the University of Leiden, Marinus van IJzendoorn and Marian Bakermans-Kranenburg, worked with Israeli scientists to compare data on a group of Jewish people who had emigrated from Poland to Israel *before* the Second World War to data on a group that did so *after* 1945. The first group hadn't experienced the Holocaust and the second had. Data on around 55,000 people in total was examined, most of whom had passed away by the time of the study. What did the researchers expect to find? That the Holocaust survivors generally hadn't lived as long as the others. After all, they had suffered through constant stress, hunger, and lack of medical care during the Holocaust. But to the researchers' surprise, they found the opposite. Those who had experienced the genocide lived on average a good six months longer.[1]

Serious illness, the death of a loved one, getting fired, a terrible accident: these events are tragedies. Yet, in the words of psychologist and trauma researcher Richard Tedeschi, they often also sow "the seeds of new life." Tedeschi emphasizes that there is nothing enviable about experiencing trauma. But he writes that almost all the people to whom he's spoken about traumatic events—parents who had lost a child, people who had lost everything in a natural disaster, who had been raped or had been disabled by an accident—had found after a period of pain, that they'd gained something big. Their trauma had changed them. They had gained a new, more balanced view of themselves and the people around them, of life and of what's important.

The New York psychiatrist William Breitbart has this to say about post-traumatic growth: "Suffering is probably necessary to make us grow. The need to find meaning is a primary force, but we may need to be confronted with our own mortality for that to occur."[2]

The fact that some systems and organisms are built to bounce back stronger from setbacks, disturbances, and irregularities suggests that a quest to achieve perfect stability, and to exercise control over uncertainty, can be counterproductive. Efforts to eradicate all risks, to create perfect systems and mechanisms that will not be subject to uncertainty and upheaval, will often do more harm than good. It weakens antifragile resistance.

Take the case of the human body; it is exceptionally antifragile, possessing fascinating self-healing mechanisms. And why not? After all, we've got billions of years of successful evolution behind us. This is why doctors learn at the start of their training that sometimes the best thing for them to do is to do nothing.

Consider a forest that's kept neat and tidy, with all the dead trees and branches nicely cleared away. It will become less thick with trees and other plant life, and less hospitable for animals, while a forest that's left alone can exercise its natural antifragility. Branches and trunks felled by storms provide nutrients and shelter; the damage and decay generate new life. Nature benefits from misfortune.

Further on in this book I'll explain how antifragility can be optimized by flip thinking, even by a strategy as simple as just waiting rather than diving in to tackle a problem. For now, let's check in again on marathoner Derek Clayton.

In 1969, two years after he became the first man to run a marathon in under 2 hours and 10 minutes, Clayton was injured again, this time while training for the Antwerp marathon. After another enforced rest period, he once again broke his personal record, and the world record, with a time of 2 hours, 8 minutes, and 33 seconds, a record that stood for no less than 12 years.

Stuck thinking

How we are prone to turn a problem into a disaster

*I would not dream of belonging to a club that
was willing to have me as a member.*
—Groucho Marx

Imagine that you've got a lot of work to do; actually too much.
A problem. So you really crank up your productivity and get
everything done in less time than it should have taken. Sounds
great. Problem solved, you might say. But your boss is likely to
think: "Excellent employee, I'll give her some more work."

So it goes with what I call "stuck thinking," which is the opposite of flip thinking. Whereas flip thinking transforms a problem into an opportunity, stuck thinking turns a problem into a
disaster. The harder we work to "solve" a problem, the bigger it
becomes. It's like when your car is stuck in the mud and you
press harder on the accelerator. The more the wheels accelerate,
the deeper in you sink.

Where else might we see stuck thinking? Trying to put a fire
out by blowing on it; angrily tugging on a tangled fishing line;
thrashing around violently to try to get out of quicksand; trying
to clear the water in an aquarium that's swirling with sand by
pushing the sand downwards; trying to get rid of head lice by

washing your hair more and more often (lice love clean hair); scratching an itch; relying on Dutch courage in order to relax in a social setting (potentially leading to drunkenness, embarrassment, and therefore more anxiety about the next social event).

But why am I focusing on stuck thinking? Why not just focus on flip thinking (after all, that's the name of the book)? Well, there are two important reasons. First, we've got to be alert to the tendency toward stuck thinking in order to avoid its traps. As with putting the cart before the horse, we've first got to get the cart out of our way. If we're blocked by stuck thinking, there's no point in trying to flip-think.

Second, stuck thinking doesn't only perpetuate problems that simply happen to us; it often *causes* our problems. By force of logic, in order to flip-think these problems, we must therefore know how to stop our stuck thinking.

Say a strict boss expects perfection from his employees, and when they make mistakes, he is furious. What is the result? The stress causes them to make more mistakes than they otherwise would. Now let's say that the boss still wants perfection but he stops getting angry. The employees become more relaxed and make fewer mistakes. Is the boss flip thinking? No, not yet. He's not yet creating an opportunity from a problem. But now that he's taken off the stuck-thinking shackles, he and his team are free to loosen up and give flip thinking a good shot.

So, how can we catch ourselves when we're stuck thinking? Most of us already have a pretty good understanding that we have a tendency toward stuck thinking. We've read plenty about how people get caught in vicious cycles. Dieticians have showcased the yo-yo effect in attempts to diet. Politicians inveigh against "revolving-door criminals." Economists warn about stock buying and selling frenzies. Our language is teeming with phrases referring to stuck thinking—"from the frying pan into the fire" and "banging your head against a brick wall" are prime examples.

We've all experienced the irony of engaging in more of precisely the behavior we'd like to stop. How do actors respond to a director who angrily shouts at them "Be spontaneous!"? They become even stiffer. If a woman says to her husband, "I'd love it if for once you'd bring me flowers on the spur of the moment," she's set herself up for continuing discontent. Now, she'll never see her husband as having spontaneously thought to buy her flowers; she'll always think he's acting on her command. What about a mother who tells her child, "You have to be independent" (thereby imposing a lack of independence on him about . . . independence); a boss who sighs to his employees, "You have to take more initiative, and dare to make mistakes" (taking their agency in deciding to entertain more risk away)? Think of media outlets that cover discussions about how an unimportant issue is receiving too much attention. Or consider the professor who drones on about the importance of interactive dialogue in a two-hour monologue.

Still, the tragedy is that we so often don't see that we're caught in stuck thinking while we're in the midst of it. As with the story of the fish who, when asked about the water they're swimming in, responds, "What water?," we're generally not aware of our own behavior. So we end up often thinking ourselves into a corner. If we try to control our thoughts by telling ourselves, "I can't think about that," we ruminate about that thing even more. What happens if you tell yourself, "When I give my presentation, I have to be relaxed"? You become more anxious. After hours of tossing and turning while trying to get to sleep, does it ever help to berate yourself with: "You really have to go to sleep now!"? Think of the completely paradoxical conclusion some people come to that they're so busy they simply don't have time for burnout (which they're already experiencing anyway). And finally, what if you're convinced that the people who love you don't see you for who you really are? How self-defeating! So, people who *don't* love you *do* see you correctly? That way of thinking couldn't be more self-defeating.

But let me emphasize here that, in order to learn to flip-think, it's important not to see stuck thinking as "bad" or "wrong" in itself. We all engage in it. Constantly. Inevitably. We're not bad or wrong for doing so; it's just how our brains work. We've got to learn not to beat ourselves up for it, or subject ourselves to our own personal witch trials. You know, the dunking tests whereby if a suspected witch floated, she was confirmed as a witch and was sentenced to death, but if she drowned she was not a witch. Unfortunately, the result was the same either way. If we beat ourselves up about our stuck thinking, we're dunking ourselves into its muck. We need to understand stuck thinking so we can intervene in the process, and then choose to flip-think instead.

Although stuck thinking is simple to define—turning a problem into a disaster—it's much more difficult to catch ourselves doing it. Two reasons why merit special attention: compensatory feedback and delayed reactions. Let's start with the first one.

Often, our ways of dealing with problems would be perfectly logical *if* they didn't provoke pushback effects. Think about a kindergarten teacher trying to get a class of children's attention by speaking louder. The children may respond by talking louder too. A rookie teacher might try to solve this by speaking even louder again, to which the kids respond in kind again, and the class breaks out in mayhem. The teacher and children form a system with a negative feedback loop of cause, effect, and cause, a vicious cycle, like a snake biting its own tail. Systems theory has a great term for this kind of pushback: compensatory feedback. Sometimes compensatory feedback escalates a problem, and sometimes it just brings a problem back to its original state, like when you put a dent in a plastic bottle and a bit later the plastic pushes back out. In these cases an intended solution to a problem is neutralized by the opposing reaction. You're back to square one.

Learning to recognize that you're caught up in a compensatory feedback system is crucial luggage for our flip-thinking journey. The driver of a car can form a compensatory feedback system with an airbag. How so? Well, the perception of increased safety due to airbags could lead to more reckless driving. Similarly, paving over dirt roads in mountain areas can lead to an increase of accidents on those roads, as drivers become careless in perceiving the roads to be safer. People who buy low-energy lightbulbs tend to leave them on more, and people with energy-saving washing machines are more likely to pop in a small load of washing.

Compensatory feedback can be quite tricky to spot. Say a company CEO tells his employees that they shouldn't work themselves to death, but they know he works 60 hours a week. His words will be canceled out by the negative example he sets.

One reason it can be hard to recognize when we're in such a negative feedback system is that pushback is often *delayed*. Think of the plastic bottle again. Sometimes a dent doesn't spring back immediately, but rather some time later you suddenly hear a little pop! and voilà!, the bottle is restored. Or consider a car company that incentivizes sales in the fourth quarter by offering fantastic discounts. Great, sales for the year get a big boost. The company celebrates a great year; the champagne corks are popping and everyone heads into the end-of-year holidays with a great sense of pride. But then sales collapse in the first quarter of the new year. What's more, as time goes on the positive effect of the discounts is further neutralized because buyers anticipate the end-of-year deals and hold off purchasing until then. This is the problem with delayed reactions: today's solutions often cause tomorrow's problems.

Sometimes compensatory feedback takes years to become obvious, as in the case of Prohibition in the US. Not long after the Civil War, alcohol was shown to do "more harm than good," leading to accidents, domestic violence, people losing jobs. The temperance movement first worked just to close saloons, but as it grew in strength there were increasing calls for a general prohibition. On January 16, 1920, the Eighteenth Amendment to the Constitution, banning the manufacture and sale of alcohol, went into effect. Consumption of alcohol dropped to less than a third of its original levels. Crime decreased and the economy improved. Even the most hardened opponents, the so-called "Wets," acknowledged the law was a resounding success. Then the tide turned. Negative effects began emerging. Drugstores and pharmacies were permitted to sell alcohol with a doctor's prescription. The result? Millions of dollars of fraudulent sales. In addition, a black market for alcohol became the engine of a boom in organized crime, lining the pockets of the mafia. Once it emerged that alcohol-trafficking rings were forming even among schoolchildren, calls to end Prohibition began overtaking support. The Wets increased in number while the Dries lost ground, and in 1933 Prohibition was repealed.

We live in a complicated world, which is rapidly becoming increasingly complex. Commenting on the complexities of systems, award-winning medical essayist Lewis Thomas said: "When you are dealing with a complex social system . . . you cannot just step in and set about fixing with much hope of helping. This realization is one of the sore disappointments of our century."[1] Figuring out how to avoid the unintended effects of trying to solve a problem requires understanding about classic errors in reasoning.

The first of these is trying to solve a problem by simply doing away with it. Our most basic reaction to a problem is often that we just want it not to be there. Sometimes we can eliminate it, but in complex systems in particular, our efforts will often result in resistance and be counterproductive.

Often what seems like the solution becomes a new problem. And the tragedy is that the players in this self-staged drama usually don't see the pattern. Let's say that someone finds their romantic partner too distant. The solution? Closeness. They should cuddle on the couch together and talk more. But the more they achieve their desired solution, the bigger a new problem they create: their partner increasingly sees them as clingy and dependent. They feel they're not being given any space. So the partner responds with their own brilliant solution, namely: keeping their distance by going out to play pool more often. Perhaps they both perceive they've worked out a good solution; but before long, let's say, somewhere between six and twelve months, their "fixes" won't be as satisfying. One will start objecting to how much time the other is out of the house and the other will see their partner as even more clingy. In some relationships, this cycle just keeps repeating, and ironically, the longer such a pattern persists, the harder it can be to spot. This may be one reason why people so often end up in similar patterns in new relationships.

Underlying this mistake of reasoning is a method of problem solving that can be hugely effective; heck, it arguably brought us the Industrial Revolution and all its benefits—namely mechanistic "cause-and-effect thinking." It assumes a straight line between cause and effect, which is why it's also known as linear thinking.

A basic premise is that every problem has a cause, and that you can find this cause by making a diagnosis. If the diagnosis is correct, you can then solve the problem with a well-formulated treatment plan. With actual monocausal problems—like a flat tire—the process works just fine. Spot the puncture. Patch the puncture. Done.

We humans have solved so many problems this way. Broken leg? A cast! Bacteria? Antibiotics! Floods? Build dykes. This method has been overwhelmingly successful. You might say we've built the whole of civilization with it. But this way of thinking is limited, even counterproductive, when it comes to more complex systems. Just think about a marriage; so many variables affect it—career ambitions, feelings about having children, ideas about happiness and mutual respect, relationships with family and friends. So if a marriage is in trouble, it can be almost impossible to pinpoint exactly what "the cause" is. There's almost certainly a complex combination of factors. But so often, we prefer to find "the cause." "He met someone else." "They were sick of each other." "Our personalities clashed." A good couples counselor knows otherwise and will point out that the problem usually doesn't lie with one or the other partner, but in the complex patterns of behavior they have developed together. Unraveling those patterns, woven over the years, requires a much more complex process of analysis than merely finding "the cause" does. The misery of the modern age is that we are faced with more and more highly complex problems, such as global warming, with multiple causes.

So many of these reasoning errors contribute to stuck thinking. There's treating the symptoms rather than the cause, like taking care of the awful beeping coming from a cardiac monitor in intensive care by unplugging the machine. Then there's assuming that a punishment will prevent bad behavior—like the

Israeli day-care managers who decided to fine parents who were late picking up their children. What was the result? Lots of additional parents started picking their children up late. How come? The fine gave legitimacy to being late: the parents interpreted it as a form of payment. Also common is letting our fear that a problem might arise cause it to happen—known as the "self-fulfilling prophecy." Suppose that some parents are scared their son will go off the rails. They are constantly checking on him, asking him if he's studied and what he's been doing. He becomes so resentful that what happens? That's right. He goes off the rails.

The ironic results of our stuck-thinking approaches to problem solving never cease to amaze. One last case: a potential homebuyer lists all the negative aspects of a property to the seller in the hope of pushing the price down. What happens? The seller comes back to the prospective buyer with a higher price. Huh?! The seller's experienced realtor knows that only someone who's really interested in buying a property would go to all that trouble.

So what insights can we draw from all our stuck thinking? Well, quite a few. First, we have to be careful not to be too quick to celebrate solutions as being successful. There's a high chance that the underlying problem persists, that we've only treated the symptoms, and that over time, we'll encounter some kind of pushback. Also, sometimes trying even harder to solve a problem only makes it worse, because our solution is part of the problem. If you feel like you're pushing a boulder up a hill, or beating your head against a wall, stop and think: which opposing forces are at work? Where and why is the system pushing back? Stop solving. Often just stopping what you've been doing is half the solution.

Second, in assessing a problem, think in terms of the complexity of systems and look for more than a simple cause–effect diagnosis. In the words of scientist Edward Lorenz, a pioneer of chaos theory, "The flap of a butterfly's wings in Brazil can set off a tornado in Texas months later." Intervening in complex systems can lead to all sorts of unexpected consequences.

Finally, acting impulsively leads to stuck thinking almost by definition. As I'll soon show you, flip thinking calls for patience in addition to creativity.

The good news? When we recognize that we are stuck thinking in a particular situation, it's often a sign that we can flip-think it. Once you've seen that you're turning a corkscrew further into a cork, you can easily get it out again by turning it the other way. Flip thinking is sometimes nothing more than reversing stuck thinking. By way of illustration, let's return to the couple we discussed earlier: one of them wanted more quality time together and the other wanted more space. Breaking the negative pushback loop might be quite simple, and (as always with flip thinking) paradoxical. Both could take the initiative, independently of each other. He (wanting more space) could complain that they see too little of each other and then push her to go out on a number of dates, spend hours with her on the couch, and send lots of texts and emails to her, and she'll likely start to feel she needs space and end up telling him, "Oh, go and play your pool!" with irritation. The same is true of the other way around. She (wanting more quality time together) could complain that she's feeling like she needs some time away from him and announce that she's going camping for two weeks, better yet with a friend named Chris. ("Who's Chris?!" he'll wonder. "A friend or a romantic rival?") She could then not call him at all while she's away. There's a good chance that when she gets home, he'll be all for some more togetherness.

Of course, such pattern-breaking interventions are no guarantee for happiness, but maintaining an unconstructive pattern *is* a guarantee for unhappiness.

stuck thinking

Stuck thinking (stuck thought, Yes-but)

Way of thinking by which problems continually increase, go from bad to worse, e.g. stuck-think himself, get tangled up in his own thinking; compare opposite, flip thinking, turning problems into opportunities.

The interim director concluded that the organization was constantly stuck thinking itself; the suspect's lawyer said that his client had stuck-thought himself in his relationships with women since his earliest childhood; the mediator helped both parties by examining the stuck-thinking process.

The four questions

On asking the right question at the right time

Complexity is the absence of simplicity.
—Edward de Bono, *Simplicity*

There is one final, crucial insight that we need to pack for our journey, namely, that not every problem should, or can, be flip-thought. The trick is to know which problems are flip-thinkable and when. To help you with this, I've developed the four questions of flip thinking. Each time you're confronted with a problem, you can use these four questions (in order) as a checklist to assess how best to approach it. The four questions are:

1. What is the problem?
2. Is it really a problem?
3. Are you the problem?
4. Is the problem the intention?

Question 1. What is the problem?

This first question sounds deceptively simple. Yet putting your finger on a problem is often (much) more difficult than it seems.

Recall that a problem always consists of a discrepancy between facts on the one hand and expectations on the other. In order to be able to define a problem, therefore, the trick is to be able to identify both the facts and the expectations involved—accurately. This is easier said than done. Suppose your problem is "My child is overactive and it's a real hassle." You might break that down into the expectation that "I'd really like a bit of peace" and the fact that "My little boy runs around the house all day long." But this is far too simple a description of the situation, leaving all sorts of questions unanswered. Exactly how active is the boy? How exactly do you define "overactive"? How exactly do you define "peace"? Is he so active at school too? Is he mostly active after meals? Does he sleep well? Does your partner also think he's overactive? In short, before you can begin solving any problem, you must describe it *adequately*.

Suppose you take a more serious look at how active your son is. You might learn that by comparison to most young boys he's actually not all that active. Or perhaps you'll discover that you've been unconsciously looking for problems with your son that you can tackle so you can prove to yourself, or others, that you're an attentive and effective parent. In that case, you can immediately move on to a new problem—what exactly does being a good parent involve? In both events, the original problem has vanished. Evaporated. On reflection, it turned out not to exist. It was a blurrily defined and, ultimately, fictitious problem.

Note that I chose the word "adequate" carefully here, because a *complete* description is not only impossible, but unnecessary. We tend to think that we can discover "the causes" of any given problem. After all, we're taught to think this way. In school we're asked questions like "What are the five main reasons the Nazi Party gained power in Germany in the 1920s?" and "What are the three most important reasons that the former Eastern

Bloc came to an end?" How wildly simplified; as if the world works like a kind of clock, and we can break events down into mechanistic explanations. But as we have seen, problems often arise out of complex systems, in which many variables interact with one another. Boss humiliates employee, employee lashes out at partner, partner yells at child, child kicks dog, dog bites cat. Systems have all sorts of ripple effects. So aim for adequate, not comprehensive.

Keeping this in mind can be especially important when it comes to painful problems. We're often inclined to conduct an exhaustive search for explanations for the most painful problems. However sensible this search may sound, it's often more an unconscious attempt to avoid having to do anything about a problem. After all, as long as you don't know exactly what is causing a problem, how can you be expected to solve it? This is why people can spend years taking life-change courses, or undergoing therapy, without making much, if any, progress.

So, limiting yourself to an adequate definition of the problem, you move on to the next question: what you think you can or should do about the problem. There are really only three good choices: you can solve a problem, let it go, or flip-think it. Not every problem needs to be flip-thought. While you could flip-think the problem of a flat tire—great, I don't have to ride to the gym today—you could also fix the tire. There's nothing wrong with solving problems; it's often the best strategy. But often problems really are simply too complicated. Sometimes they're too complicated to flip-think too. This is when you've got to resort to the third option: let the problem go.

Say you live next door to an airport and the noise really bothers you but you can't move. Then you have a problem that can be neither solved nor flip-thought. The noise bothers you, and there's no opportunity to discover in that. What is letting go then? I don't mean that you can let go of the problem in the sense that it won't bother you at all anymore. No. What I mean is that you let go of trying to find a solution. You accept that there is a problem and that you can't do anything about it. It's crucial to understand that this is not the equivalent of doing nothing about a problem, which people commonly do. Letting go is an affirmative decision to accept the problem. Without that, the problem will increasingly weigh on you. You'll keep hearing that little voice in your head that tells you to "deal with it." You'll grow more and more annoyed about it and frustrated. But if you let it go, over time its effect on you will lessen. You'll stop fuming every time you hear an airplane take off.

So, to summarize, once you've adequately defined the problem, ask yourself if you can solve it. If so, great; solve it. Problem gone. If not, can you flip-think it, or do you have to let it go? Only if you think that the problem can be flip-thought do you proceed to question 2.

Question 2. Is it really a problem?

This second question concerns the *urgency* of the problem. Is it a problem with a capital P or is it just a bit of a snag? Our brains are very good at creating the proverbial mountain out of a mole-hill. We love to complain about problems, and we see them everywhere. So, it's raining. Is that *really* a problem? Does it truly deserve our attention? But that's an easy one. How bad is it that you regularly have serious conflicts with your teenage daughter? We've come to expect an impossible perfection in our lives, and it's interesting to ask whether it's this tendency that is much more the problem than our litany of perceived problems. Shouldn't we treat minor annoyances, inconveniences, and daily frustrations as a natural part of life? Take the case of marriage. As psychologist Jeffrey Wijnberg writes, "Simply being satisfied is suddenly not enough anymore, so spouses sign up for couples counseling as soon as communication isn't absolutely flawless." Now don't get me wrong, but I would say communication issues are a defining feature of marriage. They're better viewed as reasons to laugh than problems to fix. Married couples forget all too quickly that they can count themselves lucky to know someone in the world who wants to live with them under the same roof. That, in itself, is reason enough to be incredibly thankful. Just think of all the lonely souls who would be happy to have someone to argue with.[1]

The trick is to be able to distinguish the small worries, which if not focused on will mostly disappear on their own, from the big ones. Your son smoked weed? Okay, but it was just the once. Who cares? I'd worry more if he *didn't* try things. The cat scratched the side of your couch, is that a disaster? No. Of course not. These are just ordinary worries, the daily hassles that are intrinsic to life. As the saying goes, shit happens.

In essence, we have the power to determine what we view as significant problems, like a chronic disease accompanied by daily pain, the sudden death of a loved one, or a sick child, versus those that are irrelevant. This second question can save you so much time and hassle. But if your answer to it is yes, and you're confident about that, it's time for the third question.

Question 3. Are you the problem?

This is the most intriguing of the four questions. Almost every time we're confronted with a problem, we perceive it as coming at us from out in the world. Problems come *to* you, not from within you. But (surprise!), thanks to our examination of stuck thinking, we now know that our expectations are an essential part of a problem. Sometimes they're the entire problem. The good news being that we can adjust our expectations. Rather than expecting our little boy to play quietly, we can expect him to spend lots of time being "lively." So often, by adjusting our expectations, problems evaporate.

The same applies to our behavior. Our actions are often contributing factors in our problems. This can be hard to admit, but if we stop doing whatever we've been doing about a perceived problem, quite often the problem falls away.

Question 4. Is the problem the intention?

If our problem has made it past the third question, we're in flip-thinking territory. The problem is real, and it therefore offers possibilities for solution. We can shift our energy from trying to combat the problem to working to tap its potential. I consider this counterintuitive question—is the problem the intention?—to be the Miracle Question of Flip Thinking. At first the question sounds absurd. How can a problem be "the intention"? Problems are annoying, aren't they? But by asking ourselves this question we help ourselves to get out of the thinking pattern that a problem by definition is something we don't want. The question helps us to stimulate our creativity to open new paths of thinking.

For example, losing your hair is something many people view as a problem. Something you don't want. But with the help of this fourth question—how could this be the intention?—you might stumble upon the idea to embrace being bald as desirable. An idea that isn't that strange. How attractive would Andre

Agassi, Dwayne Johnson, or Michael Jordan be if they weren't bald? Their "problem" became the intention.

In the next part of the book, I'll introduce you to 15 strategies for flip-thinking problems into opportunities. While each strategy is fundamentally based on saying "yes" to reality, accepting a problem, and *moving with it* toward an unexpected possibility, they operate differently and each is better suited to some problems than others. Assess each one by one, think about how you might be able to apply it in your life, and start giving them a whirl.

Enjoy the ride.

Wrap-up

And with that our luggage is packed.
In total we've got seven items:

1. Accept reality

A number of things in life are unchangeable. Like the blowing of the wind. Stop investing energy in trying to change them. The joke is that accepting the unchangeable can sometimes lead instantly to a new opportunity.

2. Observe carefully

We see what we think we see, not what's there. Our perception is necessarily incomplete and biased. It's a truism, but it's very important. After all, facts are the core of flip thinking. They are the lever between the problem on one hand, and the opportunity on the other.

3. Assume that problems don't exist

Problems are the tension that we feel between what is and what should be, the gulf between dream and reality. Throw the shutters open, take a look with fresh eyes. Let go of what "should be" and observe what is. Reality contains only facts. Problems are in our heads.

4. Learn to live with stress and instability

One of the biggest obstacles to flip thinking is our contentment. "It's fine like this, isn't it?" we think. But good is the enemy of great. Flip thinking thrives best in an attitude of constant renewal.

5. Make use of antifragility

People, organisms, and systems can be antifragile: they have the ability to grow when faced with adversity. They are able to incorporate problems and even to improve thanks to them. Adapting when encountering difficulty is one of nature's inherent characteristics. One of the most efficient ways to make use of antifragility is non-intervention, not doing: let the power of self-repair work its wonders.

6. Stop stuck thinking

The world is full of complex systems, and in many cases when we try to change or "fix" them, they push back, with compensatory feedback that negates our attempts. The pushback may be delayed, sometimes even for years, it may show up somewhere unexpected in the system. Stuck thinking is when we persevere with trying to solve a problem in these ways that actually end up having a negative effect (e.g. working late to get through your unsustainable workload—only to have your boss then further *increase* your workload). Flip thinking requires the ability to recognize patterns of stuck thinking and to stop them.

7. The four questions

Not every problem can or needs to be flip-thought. Some problems can just be solved. Other problems are so complex, or you have so little influence on them, that you have no choice but to let them go. Only once you've answered the first three questions about your problem—What is the problem? Is it really a problem? Am I the problem?—do you know it's suitable to face the fourth question—Is the problem the intention?—and that it's ready to be flip-thought.

PART 2

The Journey

Four basic attitudes

Love, work, battle, and play

It would be naive to approach the world with just one basic attitude. Sometimes optimism is needed; at other times perseverance, cunning, creativity, or patience is required. I've grouped the 15 flip-thinking strategies into four *basic attitudes* you can use to engage with reality. These are: love, work, battle, and play.

When you are faced with a situation that you want to flip-think, always start by asking yourself what attitude is required: does it call for love and attention, or should you gear up for a fight? Will it require hard work, or perhaps a playful approach would be most effective?

We are often intuitively aware of which of these attitudes is best in any given situation. We'll tell ourselves, "Lighten up about it," or "You've got to concentrate." Trust your instincts—flip thinking is a combination of logic and intuition. Once you have worked out which attitude is best for the situation, you can go on to choose an effective strategy.

Love

Strategies 1 to 4

The strategy of acceptance

The strategy of waiting

The strategy of amplifying

The strategy of respect

Strategies that use love as their starting point rely on the good in people, the positive opportunities offered by the current situation, and the hopeful belief that circumstances can change for the better. The key elements of these strategies are acceptance, reconciliation, and patience.

The strategy of acceptance

When we act in harmony with things,
we meet the least resistance.

In *Raiders of the Lost Ark,* the first film in Steven Spielberg's Indiana Jones series, a scene was planned in which actor Harrison Ford, as Indy, has an intense swordfight with one of his many assailants. The fight was to be one of the film's highlights, and no fewer than three days were scheduled for filming it. In order to make the scene as convincing as possible, Ford had been practicing his sword technique and the choreography for weeks. But on the first day scheduled for filming, Ford suffered a serious attack of diarrhea and couldn't do the fight. Fortunately, Ford had a great idea. He suggested to Spielberg that it might work better not to have the fight. When the menacing swordsman flourishes his massive blade, Indiana Jones just sighs, pulls out his gun, and simply shoots his attacker. It is one of the classic scenes in motion picture history. Absolutely brilliant flip thinking!

The first, simplest, and most obvious—but at the same time perhaps the most difficult—strategy is that of acceptance. As the psychologist Carl Jung put it, "We cannot change anything unless we accept it. Condemnation does not liberate; it oppresses." The question at the heart of this strategy is: is there something I'm resisting that I would be better off accepting? The wind? Diarrhea? My mood? As the Indiana Jones story illustrates so perfectly, once we stop resisting that which we can't change, sometimes a new opportunity arises that we would never have seen if we'd kept resisting, if we had held on to how the situation "should be."

The strategy of acceptance is the first of the 15 strategies for good reason. You could look at acceptance as the *mother of all strategies*. It's the cornerstone of flip thinking; a foundation for all the other strategies. In many cases, simply accepting reality is all that's needed to make a flip.

But, of course, acceptance is easier said than done. It doesn't just mean letting go of how you think the world should be; it also requires a certain frame of mind. As long as we are judging, fretting, evaluating, coming up with scenarios about what *should* be, we're not accepting. Only by observing reality without such normative judgment can we truly accept it. As a fact. Observing reality in this way requires a particular state of mind best described as "paying attention." The essence of "paying attention" is that you strive to be present and aware in the here and now, without judging, evaluating, or trying to change reality as it is. There are no problems to be solved, worries to pay attention to, or reflections on the past or future that draw out attention. You just are aware. No more, no less.

This kind of acceptance isn't easy. That's in part because acceptance has a bad reputation. We associate it with resignation and submission. As if it's a form of weakness. And we prefer to be strong, self-assured, and autonomous. We would prefer to shape reality rather than bend to it. Yet reality is infinitely stronger than any one of us. We are just a tiny part of an immense universe. Often we act as if that one tiny part can control the universe, but of course it doesn't work like that. We are a fragile part of a larger whole.

Ironically, the illusion of control, of the power to fit reality to our design, makes us weaker. We fight hopeless battles, do our best to resist the inevitable, and often end up shutting ourselves off from possibilities we won't entertain. Resistance doesn't build our strength; it's acceptance, and then *adaptation,* that make us stronger. Adaptation is a vital creative force. We must harness it and turn it to our advantage. Plants, animals, people, everything in nature has become what it is thanks to the phenomenal capacity of adaptation. The famous phrase "survival of the fittest," coined by Herbert Spencer and adopted by Charles Darwin, is sometimes taken to mean "survival of the strongest," but that wasn't Darwin's point. Those who are the fittest, he showed, are the ones that adapt best to challenges. Animals survive best by adjusting to meet the demands of their environment. As we saw earlier, nature is antifragile. Plants that grow in dry ground are the ones that develop the deepest roots. Adaptation leads to transformation.[1]

One of the ways we can experience the positive effects of this nonjudgemental state of being is by listening to other people with acceptance. By showing people that you are sincerely willing to accept what they think and feel, you offer them recognition, which is a magic tool. This can have a transformative effect on children. Many parenting problems—and indeed most social or relationship issues—are a direct result of the fact that people don't feel seen, heard, and known for who they really are. In the words of Paul Ferrini, author of the international bestseller *Love Without Conditions*: "Love does not complain, argue, or blame. Love simply embraces the other exactly as s/he is."

The power of acceptance helped an interim manager of a group of disgruntled teachers to bring them around to his management style. They had formed a tight unit, several of them having complained to him, "Nobody listens to us." He got them all together for a special meeting. He planned to accept how they felt, to just listen to them and try to get a good understanding of their issues. One teacher said, "We want more information, we want openness, transparency," and the whole group agreed. "Does this mean," the manager asked, "that you want to see the budget, for example?" "Yes," a few of them replied immediately. "No," most of them said. They then began to discuss the matter among themselves. Then the manager asked, "Does this mean that you want to talk about the new building?" This received the same mixed response. The result? They immediately became less bonded around their resistance to him. As he had expected, the real problem was simply that they felt they weren't being heard.

Listening is key to acceptance. I knew of a young man who used this strategy when faced with a difficult landlord. The landlord would pop by regularly to ask if everything was going well and then take up lots of the tenant's time complaining about the hard life of a landlord. Meanwhile, if the tenant had a maintenance problem with the apartment, the landlord wasn't responsive. What can you do? You really want to get rid of him, but it's also in your interest to maintain good relations. In the end, having given him a friendly brush-off a number of times, the young man decided to take the time to talk to him. He offered him a coffee, the landlord talked frankly about his properties, the tenants, and everything involved. While he talked, the tenant nodded in agreement, occasionally asked a question that kept the conversation going, and commented that it's quite difficult to find a nice place to live in the city. Now, three months later, they are on friendly terms. The tenant can always call him if he needs anything, and should he want to move, the landlord has told him, "You just have to let me know, because then I can see whether I've got something nice for you for a good price."

Being a good listener is a skill that is fairly easy to learn. Every basic communication course teaches it: ask questions, which indicates interest, nod in assent and vocalize agreement periodically; don't cut people off and allow silences to fall; summarize what you've been told now and again—referred to as "paraphrasing." Knowing to do all of this, though, doesn't mean that it's easy to do, particularly if what someone is saying is irritating or contradictory to what we think they should be saying.

To see some more ways that acceptance can transform a problem into an opportunity, here is a set of stories that progress from an "easy to accept" problem to a few more challenging ones, culminating with a problem that is "virtually unacceptable." While reading them, think to yourself how you might have dealt with them. Would you have been able to accept, and to adapt?

Around 1900, tea was only available in loose-leaf form, sold in tins, and the tins were fairly pricey. Legend has it that New York tea importer Thomas Sullivan was facing stiff competition and, to save money, he decided to stop packing the tea samples he sent out to prospective buyers in tins and instead use silk bags, which were considerably cheaper than tins. While Sullivan considered the bags only as alternative packaging, he learned from some customers that they were using the bags for dunking the tea in place of metal infusers when they complained that the silk was too finely woven to be a good infuser. Rather than explaining to them that he hadn't intended that the bags be used that way, Sullivan accepted their behavior and came up with the idea of using a more loosely woven gauze fabric in place of silk, thereby developing the teabag as we know it today.

What an opportunity Sullivan spotted, just by not immedi-

ately objecting in response to his customers' criticism of the
bags. So simple and yet so difficult. Accepting opportunities is
an art. If you look back on your life, how many opportunities
might you have let slip past you? We've all done so, for so many
reasons; because pursuing an idea would have caused too much
turmoil in our life, because we haven't wanted to give up the
security of our current job; but also so often because we failed
to perceive what seemed to be a problem as an opportunity.
Well, good for Sullivan, you may be thinking, but after all his
customers led him to his insight. Okay, let's consider a trickier
case.

How would you respond if you ran a business that was confronted with widespread customer theft? Would you accept it?
On first-class flights with Richard Branson's airline Virgin Atlantic, the meal is accompanied by distinctive salt and pepper
shakers. They're shaped like little planes and are called Wilbur
and Orville, after aviation pioneers the Wright brothers. Passengers are crazy about them. So crazy, in fact, that many of
them can't resist the temptation to allow the shakers to "fall"
into their hand luggage.

So many people were taking them that replacing them was a
considerable expense, and Virgin Atlantic's financial department wanted to get rid of them. But Branson was not at all keen
on that. Why get rid of something so popular? Rather than taking them out of circulation, he had the text "pinched from Virgin Atlantic" added to the shakers. The result? Wilbur and
Orville still get stolen, but they became one of the company's
most successful promotional campaigns. As well as being a nice
souvenir, they're conversation starters, thanks to the playful
text, and market the airline. They make for a great story at dinner parties, and the good cheer Virgin showed was great for the
brand's maverick image.

Okay, let's ratchet things up further. What about accepting that sometimes you're not going to be able to change people's behavior, even if it's dangerous to them? That's what the staff of the Benrath Senior Center in Düsseldorf, Germany, were able to do. Many of their residents suffer from Alzheimer's disease, and they tend to run off from the facility, trying to make their way to their former homes, even though often they no longer have homes to return to. Of course, telling them they mustn't doesn't work; they simply don't understand. So what did the center do? It placed a fake bus stop—an exact copy of a real bus stop—just outside the grounds. Now, patients who run away can be easily found at the bus stop. Nurses approach them gently, telling them the bus is running a bit late and invite them to have a cup of coffee in the meantime. Five minutes later, the patients have already forgotten that they wanted to catch the bus. The idea was so successful that other care homes across Europe adopted it.

Now let's consider one of the most difficult things to accept— that your romantic partner has cheated on you. A dear acquaintance of mine was married with a daughter when she was confronted with the fact that her husband had gotten another woman pregnant, and the woman would be having the baby. The husband said he loved both women. I would dare to conjecture that in more than 95 percent of such cases, this would have led to a vicious conflict. Most wives would either have left him or required that he choose between them and the other woman.

My friend instead thought deeply about the essential values and principles that guided her in life, as apart from what marriage laws, social convention, or the Bible dictate about such a situation, and she took the brave step of choosing a "yes-and" life. She decided to keep her family together, did her best together with her husband to forgive him (for which he, quite rightly, had to do most of the work), accepting that her husband had a second family. This was more than 20 years ago, and now, looking back, she concludes that—despite all the difficulties she had to deal with—she made the right decision.

"But how is this really a case of flip thinking?" you may ask. Sure, it's a story of accepting, but where was the opportunity for her? What is the "and" of her "yes-and"? Well, she didn't see it herself at the beginning. As she told me, "Having two households meant that he had to divide his time between our family and the other family. At the start I could only see it as a problem, and I tried as best I could to deal with it, to bear it. But one day I was sitting at home by myself, with three days stretching ahead of me in which just my daughter and I would be at home, and I realized that I really wanted that. Suddenly I recalled that he and I had started our marriage by agreeing that we would continue to lead lives of our own as well. That was the reason that we had deliberately chosen to only have one child. I recollected that I'd been the one, in fact, who had insisted on that. He would have preferred to have had more children. But I couldn't think of anything more stifling than a marriage in which you lived in each other's pockets seven days a week and were at your children's beck and call twenty-four hours a day. At that moment, I realized that I was leading my life in exactly the way I had wanted it. Bizarre! Some people said to me, 'Yes, but now you're left looking after your daughter on your own, he's got himself off the hook too easily.' But those people don't understand that that's precisely what I wanted most. I've always loved having time alone with my daughter. And if I wanted time for my own socializing, it was never a problem. We always sorted something out. As to whether he's got himself off the hook? I don't think so. The situation was harder work for him than it was for me. That's still the case today."[2]

I realize that this story is quite an extreme example. And of course I don't mean that you should simply "accept" your partner cheating. On the contrary. But for this woman in this specific situation the strategy she chose worked for her; it's an example of acceptance in action—not an instruction. And that's what flip thinking is all about. Finding new unexpected paths of thinking and behavior that fit to *your* desires, needs, and goals. Flip thinking is not about how the world should be. It's always about how the world could be. Not in general. But for you. In your specific situation.

It must be said that accepting a situation isn't always the best option; sometimes it's absolutely essential to say a loud and clear "no" and not doing so would make one a spineless mollusk. But it's amazing how many problems can be flipped by acceptance; by adapting and capitalizing on the possibilities of what is rather than digging in about what *should* be.

The strategy of waiting

Sometimes you have to wait to create.
And often that's the most difficult thing to do.
Doing nothing.

There's an old proverb about a Chinese farmer. One day this farmer, out of the blue, came across a wild horse. "What amazing luck," the other villagers said. And the farmer answered, "Maybe." The farmer's eldest son decided to tame the wild horse. But he fell off the horse and broke his leg. "What terrible luck," the villagers said. And the farmer answered, "Maybe." Some time later, war broke out and the army came to recruit all the village's healthy young men. The farmer's son was passed over because of his broken leg. "What good luck," the villagers said. And the farmer answered, "Maybe."

Whether something is good or bad luck is partly determined by the circumstances. The strategy of waiting makes use of this insight. The world never stops moving. Something might look like a problem at one moment, but transform into a new opportunity as soon as the situation changes. Flip-thinking reality by accepting things as they are and adjusting the way we deal with them is the purest form of flip thinking. It's the most effortless, self-evident, and natural way of dealing with reality. You go along with what there is, and bide your time. That's all. The beauty of it is that it's *time*, not you, that does the work.

As an illustration: the Eiffel Tower was built as the monumental entrance to the 1889 World's Fair. The tower was a success for the period of the exposition, but after that the number of visitors fell dramatically and ultimately reached zero. Even lowering entry prices didn't help. Parisians had been unhappy about the 1,063-foot-high tower right from the start. Once it no longer served a purpose they had had enough. They thought it was a big monstrosity that was out of keeping with the rest of Paris's architecture and hogged the skyline. The structure did serve one good purpose, though; its height suited it ideally as a communications tower, so radio antennae were mounted on it. Over the years, standing there in all its ugliness, the tower became *the* symbol of Paris and a tourist magnet that attracts 6 million visitors each year.

Taoists have a term, *wu wei,* which more or less means "doing by not doing." That may sound like just kicking back and relaxing, but in fact it's an active, conscious choice to do nothing. For example, a referee of a soccer match may decide not to blow his whistle for a foul because stopping play would be against the interest of the team fouled, such as if the team is in a good scoring position. It is called the advantage rule. He lets the play go on and may call the foul a bit later. Is he doing something? Or is he doing nothing? The answer is both. He's waiting.

The strategy of waiting might seem passive, but it demands an extremely high state of alertness. The art is to know when the moment has come to take action. You could think of the strategy of waiting as dancing with reality, where *following* is more important than leading. The trick is to sense what the next move will be, to be *in sync* with the moment, and to be constantly aware of the forces that surround you. This requires being attuned to *momentum.* The waiting strategy also demands a finely tuned sense of timing. Waiting sometimes involves a real challenge of patience. Think of a farmer who has to choose when to harvest his wheat. If he acts too soon, the grain won't be fully mature, but if he waits too long, the grain will get too dry and he'll lose lots of yield. When the strategy of waiting is applied optimally, you're like a wise farmer.

Doing things by deliberately not acting is not natural to us. We tend to want to tackle challenges; to roll up our sleeves and dive in. It makes us feel like we're on top of things; we've got them under control. Gabriël Anthonio, professor of leadership at the University of Groningen, offered these thoughtful comments on how misguided this is:

> Doing nothing when faced with a complex problem or issue can be a form of apathy or even neglect; that's not what we're talking about here. Attentively doing nothing is about watching, listening, and observing. If you're not involved, paying attention is precisely what makes you more involved. You consider the problem with an open mind, without prejudices or opinions. No reports are written, no actions taken, but attention is paid. That's all. My experience as a manager and professional is that many—even complex—systems can be solved by paying genuine, serious attention to them. I'm particularly talking about that category of problems for which we have to admit that, in all honesty, we simply don't know the solution (yet). But due to a modern need for "control," or other neurotic motives, we often decide to do something anyway. At the same time, everyone involved is well aware that this adds no value to the situation; on the contrary. This compulsive thinking about solutions and subsequently taking action often adds new problems to the situation. [. . .] It turns out that there's a unique force to be found in paying attention to a problem. The problem often solves itself.[1]

Yet dealing with problems by deliberately not taking action is often not valued. We're much more likely to be rewarded for the things we've done than those we've left alone. Bonuses are never given for things that aren't done; they're given for things that are demonstrable and, often, measurable. That leads to some perverse results. Take the case of a private surgeon who decides not to treat a hernia because his assessment is that the patient is very well able to heal by himself. The surgeon has confidence in the antifragility of the body. But he will be paid much less than if he decides to operate, possibly putting the patient at greater risk.

In order to encourage wise inaction, therefore, we need to redesign our reward structures. Consider that doctors in ancient Chinese villages received a fixed amount of pay each month from all the healthy people in the village. Their job, in return, was to ensure that people remained healthy, advising about nutrition and exercise, and if someone got sick, payment stopped.

Ricardo Semler, the director and owner of Semco SA, a highly successful Brazilian company, has mastered the skill of waiting and letting a situation take its course. In his book *The Seven-Day Weekend*, he tells the story of a secretary who had become a real problem. She'd been a good colleague, but had started arguing with people, and spreading nasty gossip, and constantly thundering around the office in anger. All attempts to talk to get her to change her behavior had failed. When the problem was brought to Semler's attention, what did he decide to do? Nothing. Absolutely nothing, making a deliberate choice to just wait and see. The result? As time went on, the secretary stopped behaving so badly. Everything was fine again. Nobody knew why she got so out of sorts or why she reverted to her old self again. She may not even have known herself. But does it matter? Sometimes simply leaving someone alone can be the best strategy.

Semler believes in giving people space as much as possible in his company. He's instituted a radical employee democracy system. Bureaucracy is minimal. The company doesn't even have a human resources department. Semler believes that a manager who needs assistance from human resources is a bad manager. His company has no organization chart or mission statement; meetings are not compulsory, and if no one turns up, the assumption is that the agenda items weren't very important. Staff decide their own working hours and salaries and recruit their own bosses. Does this result in chaos? Far from it. With a staff of about 3,000, turnover is minimal, and by the time Semler published his book in 2003 the company's revenue had grown from $4 million to more than $250 million. The company also weathered the credit crisis of 2008 easily. Semler now gives talks all around the world to spread his vision of leadership.

Why is waiting such an effective strategy? One reason is the way creativity works. If you want to come up with truly new opportunities (and that's what this book is essentially about), then realizing you don't have an answer at the moment, and taking a break from a problem to do something else in the meantime, often leads to a solution. Abundant scientific research supports this. For example, Professor Steven Smith of Texas A&M University conducted an experiment in which test subjects were asked to solve some puzzles. Some of the subjects were allowed to take a short break, and they turned out to be significantly faster at solving the puzzles. What's more, the longer the break, the faster they found the solutions. The break was especially effective when the researchers had helped the subjects by giving them a hint when they gave them the puzzles. Both groups were given the same hint, but the group who were given more time were able to make better use of the hint. The conclusion drawn is that information often needs to be processed subconsciously, or you could say incubated.[2]

A great deal has been written on the "a-ha" experience, a moment of sudden insight. All interesting literature on this emphasizes the importance of waiting. Good ideas take time; they have a gestation period. In order to make optimum use of our subconscious problem solving, we should feed our minds all the information about a problem we can and then relax—maybe sleep a bit, take a bath, go for a walk, or just daydream. The subconscious will be working away, like a buzzing network server silently performing complex calculations. Then suddenly an idea will come bubbling up, seemingly out of nowhere. Voluminous accounts of such "a-ha" moments have been told by scientists and artists, and they all follow the same pattern: the brain was given a task, this was followed by a break from working on it, and then, boom, the insight appeared.

Rita Levi-Montalcini, joint winner of the 1986 Nobel Prize in Physiology or Medicine, described the experience this way: "You've been thinking about something without willing to for a long time. Then, all of a sudden, the problem opens to you in a flash, and you suddenly see the answer." Konrad Lorenz, joint winner of the Nobel Prize in Physiology or Medicine in 1973, also stressed the importance of waiting. "[You keep] all human facts afloat, waiting for them to fall into place, like a jigsaw puzzle. And if you press . . . if you try to permutate your knowledge, nothing comes of it. You must give a sort of mysterious pressure, and then rest, and suddenly BING!, the solution comes." George Spencer-Brown, mathematician and philosopher, explains in his book *Laws of Form*: "To arrive at the simplest truth [. . .] requires years of contemplation. Not activity. Not reasoning. Not calculating. Not busy behavior of any kind. Not reading. Not talking. Not making an effort. Not thinking. Simply bearing in mind what it is one needs to know."[3]

The French mathematician Henri Poincaré related how the

solution to a stubborn problem came to him only after he set out on a journey and was forced to put his work aside for a few days. "The changes of travel made me forget my mathematical work. Having reached Coutances, we entered an omnibus to go some place or other. At the moment when I put my foot on the step the idea came to me, without anything in my former thoughts seeming to have paved the way for it."[4] Mozart similarly described how the ideas for a new composition would seem to come flooding into his mind during a relaxing walk or while lying in bed, unable to sleep. He'd hear the entire composition, not in parts, but as one entire whole. And Einstein said that his best ideas came to him when he was sitting staring into space or when he was in the shower.

Until fairly recently, our subconscious mind was seen as a dark basement, a place where mostly unprocessed and traumatic experiences are stored away. This view of the subconscious has changed radically in recent years alongside developments in the field of psychology. Neurological research shows that far and away the largest portion of our thinking is subconscious. Ap Dijksterhuis, a Dutch social psychology professor specializing in the subconscious, even states that the ratio of conscious to subconscious thinking is 1:200,000. To express that in terms of distance, if our consciousness was a meter, then the subconscious would be about equal to the distance from London to Bath in England.

We can perform the most complex skills without needing to give them conscious thought. Think of how we can drive for minutes at a time absentmindedly and then "wake up" with a start when a cyclist or a child suddenly approaches the road. The interesting question is: who or what is it that makes us wake up at that moment? It's not our consciousness; that was off somewhere else. In the same way, we can ask: who or what caused Poincaré to come up with an insight while stepping on to the bus in Coutances? Did he "think of" that insight? Obviously not—he wasn't thinking at all. He received it, from his subconscious. If we learn to have more faith in this intuitive intelligence, we gain greater access to an inexhaustible source of creativity. After all, our species was wildly successful for tens of thousands of years of evolution without language or higher-order conscious thought. In order to tap the power of our subconscious, the skill of waiting is particularly important. The more we put pressure on ourselves to solve complex issues in a short space of time, the worse the outcome often is.

The strategy of waiting is in one way the easiest, but it can be difficult to practice because our impulse to act on a problem is so strong. So keep in mind the wisdom of the farmer from the Chinese proverb, who waited to see whether an unruly horse, or a son's broken leg, might reveal their silver linings in time.

The strategy of amplifying

The guy who invented the first wheel was an idiot.
The guy who invented the other three, he was a genius.
—Sid Caesar

Let's say that a company has just carried out its first customer-satisfaction survey. The survey shows that 93 percent of customers are satisfied to very satisfied. What else should the company want to know?

The third flip-thinking strategy, *amplifying,* looks at what's going well and how you can build on that. So, in essence: look at what's working, and keep doing it. But despite—or perhaps because of—the fact that it's such a simple strategy, I dare say that it's the most underrated of all the strategies in this book. A lot of people make the serious mistake of thinking that if something's simple, then, by definition, it can't be clever. Another reason this strategy is so often underrated is not because we don't understand it or can't apply it, but because we are so concerned with what's not working—the problems and hitches—that we often overlook what is working.

Let's go back to the matter of the customer-satisfaction survey. It indicates that 7 percent of customers are *not* satisfied. Shouldn't the company focus on figuring out why? Then it could reach 100 percent satisfaction, or close. Well, let me ask you, might it not be more fruitful to examine why 93 percent *are* satisfied and to focus on doing more of what they like? You might even discover that you're unintentionally or accidentally doing something they just love.

We focus so often on trying to solve problems by looking for the cause. For example, you might try to cure a disease by looking for its causes; this could be a virus or bacteria. Once you have determined the cause you could try to eradicate it. Kill the virus. Beat the bacteria. That strategy can work very well, nothing wrong with that. This is how healthcare mostly works. Identify the disease, find the cause, remove the cause, patient better.

But when it comes to the creation of new opportunities, this approach is lacking. There's no straight line from what's gone wrong in the past to what could go well in the future. Think about it. You could also try to cure a disease by looking for people who carry a virus or bacteria but for some reason haven't developed a disease. How does their body function that it can protect itself? What can we learn from them? Sometimes there's a shorter path to success than looking for the cause of the problem: looking into what's working.

This amplification strategy involves a radical retraining of our gut instincts. We're so completely convinced that we need to find flaws and causes when there's a problem (or even when there isn't a problem—as above, 93 percent satisfaction is pretty good) that the idea of instead focusing on the things that are going well seems not only naive but irresponsible. Most people, especially perfectionists, will resist. "Look at what's going well? Ha!" they'll say. "Take a look at the huge mess going on here. I think we'd better take care of that first!"

So, let's consider where the reflex to want to know the cause of a problem comes from. Steve de Shazer, the late psychotherapist and founder of solution-focused therapy, gets right to the heart of the matter, summing up the errors of reasoning in-volved: "Causes of problems may be extremely complex, their solutions do not necessarily need to be."[1] In other words, causes of problems are often not simply the opposite of the causes of success. Nonetheless that's what we think, consciously or un-consciously. Something in us says that if we know how *not* to do something, then we automatically know how it *should* be done. That might sound logical, but it doesn't make any sense. Know-ing how to do things right is more than just understanding what can go wrong. Otherwise, you could become an Olympic champion skier by studying skiing accidents.

Focusing on our weaknesses and working to improve on them is widely considered a virtue. We call it healthy self-criticism or self-development (which has spawned a whole in-dustry of books, gurus, and events), and we think it's more admirable to focus on the things we still need to learn than on our existing talents. There's nothing wrong with attending to our deficiencies or trying to figure out why things aren't work-ing properly, as long as that doesn't lead us to overlook what's going right.

In trying to assist blind people, it's of course important to focus on the things they can't do, or can't do as easily, to develop aids to help them with those tasks. But to complement that, a flip-thinking approach would be to focus on things they *can* do. For example, blindness tends to strengthen people's other senses. One instance of this is that reading Braille builds more sensitiv-ity of touch. The German project Discovering Hands has made brilliant use of this talent. The institute trains blind women to detect breast cancer in other women at an early stage; their fin-gers are like living scanners. The result? Thanks to their height-ened sense of touch, blind women are able to detect tumors of only 4 to 6 millimeters in size, whereas well-trained doctors can usually only detect ones from 1 to 2 centimeters. The difference is vital. Early diagnosis of breast cancer often makes the difference between life and death. The project is the brainchild of German gynecologist Frank Hoffmann. A research project conducted in Austria in 2022 by Joanneum Research revealed that Discovering Hands' visually impaired palpation experts find twice as many tumors as sighted doctors. So prospects are more than promising. For all parties involved. As one of the project participants said, "For the first time in my life I'm not viewed as someone with flaws and limitations, but as someone with an exceptional talent."[2]

Research on the notion of "thinking in opportunities" is still at an early stage in psychology. Martin Seligman, one of the world's leading psychologists and a leader of the Positive Psychology Movement, points out that only one in every hundred articles written by psychologists is related to happiness. The other 99 percent relate to unhappiness, or the causes thereof. He objects to psychologists' and psychiatrists' tendency to attribute people's behavior to some pathology, even behavior that's made people successful. He cites the example of Bill Gates's performance-oriented character as being explained by a desire to be more successful than his father. This focus on the negative is, more than anything, a *missed opportunity*. Seligman says, "If all you do is take away the psychopathology, you don't get a happy person, you get an empty person."[3] He therefore argues that the core question in psychology shouldn't be "How can we make misfortune bearable?" but rather, "How can we create happiness?"

The effect of the strategy of amplifying is extraordinary. A famous study on the power of amplifying, published as *Pygmalion in the Classroom*, was carried out by Robert Rosenthal and Lenore Jacobson in 1965. They evaluated the relationship between teachers' expectations of students and the students' performance. The researchers drew up lists of children assigned to classes and randomly added totally made-up descriptions of their level of ability, along the lines of "Marie is very smart" or "John can find it a bit hard to keep up." At the beginning of the school year, the lists were handed out to the teachers of those classes. The study found that if a teacher was under the impression, due to the list, that Marie was very clever—while she was in reality a fairly average student—the teacher would have higher expectations for Marie and that resulted in higher performance. The reverse also turned out to be true. Teachers tended to focus less on children who were characterized as not particularly smart, such as by asking them fewer questions and making less eye contact with them, as well as making lower demands on them. Over time these students tended to begin to underachieve. Rosenthal's research caused quite a commotion. The correlation between the teacher's expectations and the student's performance proved so strong that these research methods are even prohibited in some countries.

The *upward* spiral of amplification—the teacher thinks the student is smart, the student behaves accordingly, the teacher's assumption is confirmed, and so on—is a great example of what system theorists call a positive feedback loop. Another example is the effect of positive word-of-mouth on increasing sales. Fashion trends are often the result of a process of continuing amplification. In these positive loops, small interventions in a system can eventually lead to massive changes, as the system constantly amplifies itself.

To provide a visual image of this amplification process, system theorists have drawn on a French children's rhyme about a pond with lily pads. Every day the number of pads doubles, and after 30 days the pond is completely covered with pads. Now, tell me, at what point was the pond half covered? Not until day 29! What was the amount of coverage on day 15, halfway through the process? The answer is disconcerting. At that point, the pond was only 0.003 percent covered. In a positive loop, a small, even almost indiscernible, initial change can produce a major outcome.

Here's another way to appreciate the effect. How many times do you think you'd need to fold in half an ordinary piece of paper—as thick as printer paper or newsprint—to make it thick enough to reach the moon? Just so you know, the distance from earth to the moon is around 239,000 miles. Have a guess. A hundred times? A thousand times? Ten thousand times? Hold that thought, I'll give you the answer shortly. . . .

Obviously *downward* spirals also occur, such as in stock-market crashes. Share prices drop and more people decide to sell their shares, which causes prices to drop further, and suddenly people in droves begin dumping shares. Because amplification can be nearly invisible for so long, often a major development seems to emerge in one fell swoop, out of nowhere, which has actually been in the works for some time. The "sudden" fall of the Berlin Wall can be explained, in part, by a process of ampli-fying discontent, stretched over many years. To many of us, the internet seemed to have suddenly appeared once the World Wide Web, and websites, had been created. But it had been in development for many years, used mainly by tech geeks. Many inventions seem to burst on the scene this way. They've been developing from a first version that causes hardly any stir and then suddenly come booming along to displace the whole mar-ket for some product. Once the fax was introduced, the telex disappeared within six months. And then the same thing hap-pened to the fax after the introduction of computers and emails. In the same way, the LP was rapidly replaced once the cassette tape emerged, and then the cassette tape was usurped once the CD gained traction, and the CD was pushed aside by illegally downloaded MP3s, which in turn were swept away by services like Spotify. Mobile telephones were of no interest to telecom companies prior to 1990. Now eight-year-olds get smartphones for Christmas, along with apps and other applications that they understand but their parents don't. The advance of cheap airline tickets for flights within Europe was barely visible until a few years back, and then all of a sudden you could fly to Barcelona and back for 49 euros. All of these "revolutionary" changes were actually the result of a process of longer-term—and for most of us, invisible—growth. Quiet, yet patient and persistent amplification. We should try to always keep in mind that after 15 days of the lily pads growing, only 0.003 of the pond was covered.

So how are positive feedback systems relevant to flip thinking? Well, accentuating the positive in them can lead to dramatic improvements in results in all sorts of areas. Wherever people work and live together, they interact to form systems, and this means that small, repeated amplifications of positive interactions can produce a massive positive effect. Management guru Tom Peters has this to say on the subject:

> Positive reinforcement [. . .] has an intriguing Zen-like property. It nudges good things onto the agenda instead of ripping things off the agenda. Our general observation is that most managers know very little about the value of positive reinforcement. Many either appear not to value it, or consider it beneath them, undignified, or not very macho.[4]

My company once gave a workshop for the staff of a high school in Veghel in the Netherlands. We asked them what they had done well recently. One of the things they said they were proud of was a somewhat unusual project. A class, which was made up mainly of students from immigrant backgrounds, had a difficult relationship with the teaching staff. The students said they were treated dismissively by teachers, and the teachers thought the students reacted defensively to their instructions. The teachers often lost their patience with the class, which the students pointed to as proof that "They don't like us." They were in a downward spiral, and the teachers decided to try and break it. They agreed that for a month they would all consistently give heartfelt compliments to the class, both to individual members and to the group as a whole. The compliments weren't fabricated; they were based on authentic recognition of positive performance. Within two weeks, they said, the atmosphere in the class had completely turned around. At the end of the school year, one of the boys said to his mentor proudly, "We're the best class they've had here in a long time, right, sir?" and the mentor could only agree.

Unfortunately, for many of us, giving positive feedback doesn't come naturally. We're trained from early on in life to focus on negatives, such as dangers we might get into. Think of the way a worried parent often speaks to their child, the stock phrases and warnings like "don't touch" and "be careful." So, from an early age, we learn to look out especially for what *isn't* good. This includes what's not good about us. We tend to focus on the things we need to improve about ourselves, and we so often do the same with others, at home and in work.

One of the best stories I came across in my research for this book is that of a major culture change at the company Avon Mexico. It's a great illustration of how, when you try to solve a problem by focusing on what *doesn't* work and start searching for the reasons for failure, you will likely end up in a negative spiral, whereas if you focus on amplifying what *does* work, you will likely kickstart an upward spiral.

For years Avon Mexico was plagued by complaints about sexual harassment by male employees, a glass ceiling for women, and a generally macho culture. A New York consulting firm was called in, but everything they tried seemed to be counterproductive. After two years of training programs the number of complaints and lawsuits had only increased. The employee evaluations of the training programs were negative, and the number of people attending workshops fell dramatically over time. The consulting firm decided to try a different tack. In 1995 they approached Diana Whitney and David L. Cooperrider, specialists in the technique of "appreciative inquiry," to help with the problem. Whitney and Cooperrider set to work asking what was working well at the company. They asked the employees who said they were satisfied with the way men and women worked together to sign up in pairs—one man, one woman—explaining that they wanted to interview these pairs about what was working well. The organization expected ten signups at the most, but hundreds of pairs responded. As a result of the conversations conducted, a whole series of proposals for improving the company culture was tried and the results were phenomenal. Were the problems solved? No, much more than that: the culture was so positively transformed that just two years later, in 1997, Avon Mexico was presented with the Catalyst Award for being the best place in the country for women to work. An unprecedented achievement.[5]

In the future, whenever you're confronting a problem, consider how you might solve it by focusing on the positives and amplifying them. Say you're trying to figure out why some people engage in criminal behavior. Why not start by focusing on why so many people follow the rules?[6]

When is applying the strategy of amplifying most effective? There are essentially three situations to which it is ideally suited. In all three, a leverage effect may be at play: a small amplification may result in a big change. First, situations in which there is a *delicate balance*. Think of a pair of scales that will lean decisively to one or the other side when just a small weight is dropped on it. This is true of many electoral contests in political systems; a tiny number of votes can make the difference between victory and defeat.

Second is situations that may require metamorphosis; a relatively sudden transition. The conditions for change may have been developing for some time, but a tipping point is reached, as when water slowly cooling will quickly turn to ice when it reaches 32°F. Social revolutions are also a good example.

The final ideal situation is when a *system* needs a positive feedback loop. Sports teams who've been playing poorly for a while may suddenly get into a winning streak once they have a winning game. The positive fan response and press lift a team's morale, the players in turn play harder and win their next game too, and so on.

Finally. Two things.

First, an example where focusing on the positive in people's behavior rather than the negative became a powerful way to encourage more of that good behavior. Visitors to the Petrified Forest National Park in Arizona were stealing a great deal of wood as souvenirs. To try to deter the theft, park officials had posted signs saying, "Your heritage is being vandalized every day by theft losses of petrified wood of 14 tons a year, mostly a small piece at a time." But the behavior persisted. In 2002, psychology and marketing professor Robert B. Cialdini, who specializes in the science of persuasion, was asked to find a way to deter thefts more effectively. He and his team came to the conclusion that the signs describing the severity and scale of the problem were counterproductive. They actually sent a message to people who wouldn't even have considered taking a piece of the precious wood that other people were doing so, and led many to think, *Why not? Everyone else does!* Cialdini and his team tested the effect of different wording for the signs, saying, "Please don't remove the petrified wood from the park, in order to preserve the natural state of the Petrified Forest." Cueing people that they could do an important public good led to significantly less theft.[7]

Last, before I forget. To help you to keep the power of amplification in mind, let's go back to my earlier question about how many times a piece of paper has to be folded in half in order to reach the moon. The answer is: just 42 times. In fact, that number would even take you 35,000 miles past the moon. Sounds crazy, right?! Just as with the lily pads, at first the height of the paper doesn't seem to be getting anywhere near being able to stretch so far. After eight folds, the height is only about 1 inch, and by 16 folds, it's only up to about 21.5 feet. But the power of doubling is such that by 40 folds you're a quarter of the way there, which means that by 41 folds, you're halfway, and voilà! One more fold and you've got your moon shot.[8]

The strategy of respect

People are ready for anything.
Apart from being taken completely seriously.

We all know them: songs—or rather, bits of songs—you can't get out of your head. The harder you try, the more they just keep popping into your mind, driving you nuts. In musicology, they're called "earworms," and University of Amsterdam musicologist Henkjan Honing points out that they're usually particularly catchy parts of songs with otherwise quite simple melodies and rhythms, which introduce harmonic tension into a song. It's best not to try to fight them. Honing's advice is to fight evil with evil. Sing the whole song *at the top of your lungs,* all the way to the end. This seems to resolve the harmonic tension and release your mind from the earworm's grip.

We've already seen that resistance often makes whatever we're resisting more of a problem and that acceptance can help us transform a problem. The strategy of respect takes acceptance a bit further. This fourth and final strategy of the "love" group has two defining characteristics. The first is that it always relates to problems with another person, or group of people. An element of human interaction is always involved. Second, the strategy goes beyond accepting some aspect of a person's behavior to actually participating in the behavior in such a way that the other person is fully aware of your acceptance. So it's not just about you accepting the person, but clearly respecting them by *showing* that you do.

Here's a great example a friend of mine, Jan, who conducts training programs in education, shared with me. He recalled, "At one school where I regularly give training sessions, there's a really nice woman who greets me, and there's something she does that I really don't like: every time, before I go into a training session, she brushes imaginary dust off my suit jacket. There's nothing really wrong with that, but it really annoyed me. It made me think of how my mother used to do that. One morning I decided to look at it differently and pretend to enjoy it. After she'd brushed my lapels, I turned around and requested: 'Do my back as well, would you please?' She gave me a funny look, but she was happy to comply. It was great, like when you're at the hairdresser and they brush hair clippings off of you. I turned around again. 'Here, do my leg too,' I suggested, lifting it up. Having fun with my ribbing of her, she cheerfully brushed off my upper leg. Before I went any further, she laughingly called time."[1]

This friend of mine really is a master in applying the respect strategy. A few years ago he bought his daughter a cat. Not even a week later, to his shock, the cat ate a fish from the neighbors' pond. The neighbor was livid, until the cat's owner said, "Well, maybe we'll have to have her put to sleep." The neighbor's fury vanished immediately. "Oh no, no, it's not as bad as all that."

The word "respect" is interpreted differently in different cultures. In some it means deference or veneration (for elderly people, leaders, or your parents), while in other cultures, it means to act with integrity in your dealings with others. At its root, however, is a meaning that's perfectly suited to our discussion of this strategy. The word comes from Latin, and is a combination of *re* (again, back, re-) and *spectare* (to look, see, view). So respecting is like being a mirror of the other person, they see themselves in you, reflected in you. They feel understood or recognized by you.

Respecting can be done in many ways. The most basic is that of *recognizing*. I mean by this that you show the other person that you accept what they think, feel, and are. Fully. Without censure, comment, or criticism. You accept the other person profoundly, and, crucially, the other person knows that this is the case. You've overtly made it clear to them. We may all have said something like, "But Dad really did love you very much, he just didn't say it." Recognizing is about Dad actually *showing* it, whether by saying it or in some other clear ways, such as with a hug. Recognition is an interactive action.

Recognizing someone is not always easy, especially when their behavior is problematic. Family therapist Téo Visser tells the story of a boy he counseled who had been arrested for smashing the windows of his house. He recalls, "I'm not a security guard; I'm here to help. I want to understand the boy. So I said to him, 'You really want to make a point about something, huh?' The boy was surprised, because he expected to be admonished. He felt that he had been recognized and he started to talk." What was the story? It turned out that his home was torn by domestic violence, so Visser told the police, and together they went to the house. "So we stepped through the broken window of the house and congratulated the parents on having such a good son," Visser continues. He made it clear to the parents that the breaking of windows was a protest against the violence in the home and a call for help. " 'Shall we talk?' I asked the parents." Listening and understanding are at the core of Visser's approach. "You don't get to that point," he concludes, "if you reprimand a kid like that and say that he's no good."[2]

Recognizing is more than respecting what someone feels and thinks—it's also about respecting how someone is. Everyone is different. We all have different temperaments, personalities, qualities, and skills. Recognizing people entails accepting all of those differences, even people's peculiarities. I love the story that was sent to my company by a mother who for years waged a fierce battle with her 13-year-old son, who had Asperger's syndrome, over changing his boxer shorts. He thought changing them daily was completely unnecessary and that it was fine to wear his for five days or longer. He was also quite fussy about which shorts he would wear. One day, shopping for new ones, the mother took him to all sorts of shops to search for some he would like, but he rejected them all. She was almost ready to give up but tried one more shop. And what did they find? A seven-pack of boxers, with each pair printed with the first letters of a different day of the week. Problem solved! These shorts recognized the son's need to live according to a fixed structure, and from then on he happily put a clean pair of boxers on every day without even being reminded.

A second form of showing respect is simply giving people what they want. This can have a very disruptive effect—especially if you give them more than they expected. Hasan Elahi is an American artist who flew into Detroit airport in June 2002 and was taken aside by the FBI for questioning, in a clear incident of racial profiling. "Where have you been?" the agent asked him. "What did you do there? Where were you on September 12?" Elahi obliged by looking up the information in his meticulously kept electronic diary. He told him that he had been teaching on September 12 and had paid the rent on his self-storage unit. "What do you have in storage?" the agent wanted to know. "Winter clothes, and some furniture I'm not using at the moment." "No explosives?" came the response. The questioning lasted an hour and a half, and Elahi answered in incredible detail due to his extensive calendar records. Finally, he was allowed to go home, but he was told to report to a local FBI office several more times over the next six months for more questioning, asking him all about his activities, down to the smallest details. He even had to undergo a lie-detector test. Eventually the questioning stopped, but the FBI asked him to let them know if he planned to travel. Rather than reacting to all this questioning with anger, which Elahi would have been totally justified in doing, he decided that he was going to respect their requests. Not only that, he decided to flip-think the situation.

He began to give the FBI more information about his doings than the agency could ever have imagined. He travels frequently for work, and for each trip, he'd call and give them his flight information. Then he started writing them emails, which over time became more and more detailed, including photos from his travels and travel tips and links to websites. Eventually he built a website on which he painstakingly recorded his activities in minute detail: including photos of his in-flight meals, of the stores where he did his shopping and the groceries he bought, and even of the toilets he visited, the gas stations where he filled up his car, and on and on. Elahi had flip-thought his way to creating a startling new form of artwork, which, in part due to a now-famous TED talk he gave about the project, has raised his profile as an artist.* He not only satisfied the FBI's demands,

---

* The joke is that, despite this mountain of factual information, you still don't know much about Hasan Elahi himself. Who is he? What motivates him? What does he think or feel? Elahi's conclusion: "The best way to maintain your privacy is to give it up."

he found a way to showcase how elaborate their questioning of him had been and make a powerful statement about how we're living in a surveillance culture. Indeed, the strategy of showing respect can be used to turn the tables on someone and throw up their bad behavior to them.

Sometimes it can be very refreshing to say an authentic, wholehearted "yes" when people ask you for something that you find inappropriate, strange, or irritating, and to which your first inclination is to say an emphatic "no," sometimes even more pleasing for you than for the other person. A teacher got in touch with me to share how she used this strategy to great effect in dealing with an unruly student. "A couple of years ago," she recounts, "when I was still working at a school for children with serious learning difficulties, I had a boy in the class who let out amazing burps." He'd unleash one about every five minutes, and the other kids loved it and started copying him. Burping became the class sport.

"I don't like burping," the teacher said. "More than that—I really hate it. But banning it didn't help. Getting cross or giving punishments didn't either. Then I came up with the idea of holding a weekly burping competition each Friday afternoon." The child who let out the longest burp would be awarded with a glass of soda in place of the vegetable juice the rest of the kids were given. "I didn't hear a single unscheduled burp for the rest of the year," she reports, "only on Friday afternoons from half past two until twenty to three. The best part is that it's taught me to burp really well too."

Of course, the effect of a surprising yes on those making inappropriate requests can also be profound. For example, when an intruder forced his way into a house in Schwanewede, Germany, and threatened the babysitter with a pistol, the two small children she was watching offered him their piggy banks.

Dumbfounded, the burglar put the pistol in his pocket and left without saying a word.[3]

A third variation of the respect strategy is to agree with a statement someone makes that you actually disagree with. This can be a marvelously effective form of mental jujitsu. The power comes from the fact that people don't always mean what they say, or aren't aware of the way what they're saying might upset others. You make use of this contradiction, as if slipping a crowbar between what they say and what they really think, which often leads to a great flip of a situation.

Consider this way the strategy could be used. A foster mother is caring for a ten-year-old foster boy and also her three-year-old birth son. Despite the seven-year age gap, the boys get along really well. But one day the foster son says to her, "If I go to another family later on or go back to my mother, that would be great, because I won't have to put up with such a rotten little brother anymore." She feels stabbed straight through the heart. How could he think that? The boys seem to have so much fun together. Instead of objecting, she bites her tongue. Later, when she's putting her foster son to bed she says to him, "I think it's really awful for you that your brother annoys you so much. Perhaps it's better if you don't play together for a week." The foster son looks at her wide-eyed and his bottom lip starts to tremble, with tears springing to his eyes. No, he responds, saying that the three-year-old is really sweet, and asking if the two of them can play together again tomorrow.

People often say things they don't really mean, in part because they assume others won't pay serious attention, or they're actually fishing for a compliment or some moral support. If someone says, "I don't think I can do it," out of politeness, we'll tend to automatically counter, "Sure you can!" If this becomes a pattern with someone, let's face it, it becomes tiresome. Next time, try to take what they're saying seriously. If the person says, "I don't think I can do it," respond with something like, "Well, yeah, it might be too much for you." Suddenly the person will start giving reasons why he or she probably can actually do whatever it is after all.

This technique also works well with the absurd, often bombastic statements people make. Trying to combat the absurdity with reason is only counterproductive. Sometimes it's better to go along with it. Consider the story of an annoying airline passenger who didn't want to fasten his seatbelt for take-off. The flight attendant asked him why, and he responded, "I'm Superman, nothing can happen to me." Showing not the least bit of annoyance, the attendant replied, "Superman would never sit here; Superman can fly himself." The man laughed and buckled his seatbelt.[4]

The comedian John Cleese—one of the members of Monty Python—told a story about the time that his mother was terribly depressed. When he said to her, "I just wish that there was something I could do. What can I do to help you?" she replied that it was very sweet of him, but that there was nothing he could do. She was simply depressed, and nothing could change that. He flipped the situation by responding, "I've got an idea. If you're still feeling this way next week I know a little man in Fulham and if you would like I could give him a call and he could come and kill you. Then you'll be dead and you won't be depressed anymore." After a short, stunned silence, she cackled with laughter. From then on he and his mother had a routine. If she was feeling down, he would ask her, "Shall I call the little man from Fulham?" and she'd answer, "Oh no, dear, I've got a sherry party on Thursday."[5]

You can also use the respect strategy to connect with people in profound and surprising ways. I worked on a theater project with homeless people as part of the Rotterdam European Capital of Culture festival in 2004, in which they told their life stories. During rehearsals, one of the participants, Francisca, became clearly stressed about the process, and one day she blurted out what was bothering her. "I think you're talking about me behind my back," she proclaimed. "I get the feeling that I don't really belong." The normal reaction would be to deny her claim, but I decided to agree. "That's right, you're right, I phone my partner every day to talk about you. Oh, and I call my mother too." "Are you winding me up?" she responded angrily. "I'm definitely winding you up," I replied, "but if you want to say that there are ducks flying over the table here, then there are ducks flying over the table. No problem." She said nothing, and I went on. "You not trusting people, maybe that's a psychological condition of some kind. I don't know; it's not my field. I do know that, even with all this fuss, you belong in this group, 100 percent." I could see that she was doing her best to stay cross, so I went further. "Look, I want to help you," I said. "How about this? Let's get everyone in a circle and they can all say why you don't belong in this group. Ready?" So everyone had their say. "I find her annoying," the first person said. "I just don't like her, that's why," said the second. Once we came full circle to Francisca, I asked, "So, what do you think, can Francisca stay?" By now she had picked up on what I was up to. In a deadly serious voice, she said, "I think she's a nasty character, but we should give her the benefit of the doubt." Loud applause erupted from the group. Then she burst out laughing. She stayed with the show, and with her tragic, moving, and bizarre life story made an indelible impression on many people.

A final variant of the strategy of respect relies on our strong psychological need for *inner consistency*. We like to see ourselves as logical, coherent, right-minded beings. We hate being called out for contradictory behavior. The judge in the trial of Mohammed B., the man convicted of the murder of Dutch filmmaker Theo van Gogh, managed to get Mohammed B. to break his silence in court with this technique. Mohammed B. had made a full confession and issued a statement saying he was prepared to take his punishment, but that he was not prepared to discuss his actions with the court. He argued that he was not accountable to the court, an institution of "the unbelieving people of the Netherlands," and he maintained a strict silence as the proceedings were conducted.

The public prosecutor, Koos Plooij, showed sincere respect for Mohammed B.'s religious principles. One day in court he said to him, "You believed that Theo van Gogh was a bad Muslim. But isn't it true that only Allah, on Judgment Day, can decide who is a good Muslim and who isn't? And if that's the case, then is it theoretically possible that Allah could judge Theo van Gogh to be a good Muslim?" After a moment of silence, Mohammed B. responded, "That's correct. In principle, I cannot and may not rule out the possibility that I was wrong." By taking the teachings of Mohammed B.'s religion seriously, Plooij was apparently able to cast some doubt into Mohammed B.'s mind about how justified the killing was.

Clearly the strategy of respect can be applied in many different ways and circumstances. Let's end on a lighter note with a humorous example. In a radio interview, Dutch comedian Brigitte Kaandorp recounted that at the start of her career, she and a female friend performed in Amsterdam's Vondelpark each week. During one of their performances, they saw a man in the bushes taking "his thing" out of his trousers, and then performing an indecent act. Shocked, the two women packed up their things and fled. A week later, at the same place, there was the same man again doing the same thing. But this time they stopped their performance and Brigitte called out cheerfully, "Ladies and gentlemen, there's a man in the bushes over there who, I believe, wants to show you something." Quick as a flash, the man put away "his thing" and fled.[6]

Work

Strategies 5 to 7

The strategy of persevering

The strategy of focusing

The strategy of rethinking

These strategies are for when a problem requires dogged determination. This type of flip thinking involves learning by trial and error, with lots of practice, persistence, and grit.

The strategy of persevering

Your best teacher is your last mistake.
—Ralph Nader

The lightbulb as we know it wasn't invented overnight. The principle of incandescent lighting was discovered around 1800. Some 40 years later, the Place de la Concorde in Paris was lit with the first electric arc lamps. But it would still be some time before long-lasting and bright incandescent lamps were available. Thomas Alva Edison took on the challenge of inventing an affordable incandescent bulb that lasted for a long time and was suitable for mass consumption. Essentially only one thing needed to be discovered yet: better material for making the filament in the lightbulb convert electricity to light. That was all. To find that material, Edison collected thousands of different materials from around the world, including all sorts of reeds and bamboo from the Amazon. His whole laboratory was packed with the strangest raw materials, and they all underwent the same process—one by one, they were carbonized and then placed carefully in a vacuum glass. Their ability to convert electricity into light was assessed. The material often fell to bits even before the power was turned on. Edison spent years testing materials this way. It was sheer drudgery. Right up until, one day, he came across: carbonized cotton. The modern lightbulb was

born. Of his many years of experimentation, Edison had this to
say: "I have not failed. I've just found 10,000 ways that won't
work."

That statement goes to the heart of the flip thinking achieved
by the *strategy of persevering*. When an experiment proves that
an idea doesn't work, then the experiment is a success.

The strategy of persevering acknowledges that problem solving is so often not a logical, linear process. It's not long division
or addition; if only it was that simple. Edison understood that
we can only come up with successful solutions by constantly
experimenting. He is the one who coined the famous saying,
"Genius is 1 percent inspiration, 99 percent perspiration." At
one point he and the chemist Martin Rosanoff were looking for
material for some kind of coating. Edison suggested working
day and night for as long as it took to find it. "But, Mr. Edison,"
Rosanoff implored him, "I've been working on it for four
months already and tried every reasonable solution, with no result." "That's just where your trouble has been," Edison replied.
"You've tried every reasonable thing. Reason doesn't work for
these types of things."

Perseverance is the strategy to resort to when you're dealing
with a stubborn problem and you have a hunch it can be flip-
thought. You've already tried everything that you could think of
that seems reasonable, and you're convinced the solution won't
come about by just accepting or waiting; you've got to actively
find it. You're at the "don't just stand there, do something" junc-
ture; so you take a gamble; take a stab in the dark.

Say you're in a relationship and you're constantly fighting, or
maybe on the contrary it's completely boring and predictable.
You've tried talking reasonably about the issues, even gone to
therapy. Do you give up and walk away? Instead you could try
experimenting with all sorts of new things that might not seem

like good ideas. Try living apart for a bit; book a vacation; maybe even explore the idea of an open relationship together. Whatever you try, you want to make an *abrupt* intervention. You're engaging in creative trial and error.* Is it working? Great! Keep it up. No? Then stop doing it and try something else. Over time you may find the relationship taking on a new luster or recharged by a new spark of attraction. You may not know exactly why. Is it important? No. You flipped the problem.

The same applies to a business that's slowly sinking into the red. You could do in-depth analysis of why things are not going well, cut back on costs, and work even harder to succeed; all seem eminently logical. But chances are they won't be much use. Those measures will likely only *delay* the failure of the business; give it a stay of execution. Instead, you could invest in three, four, five experiments, say with a new sales approach or a new product line. A simple law applies: more interventions means more opportunities. That's why McDonald's, which has one of the simplest menus in fast food, with a very limited number of dishes, runs some 6,000 experiments with new menu items each year, of which perhaps two or three might make it on to the menu long term.

Crucial to this strategy is that you try things *knowing that they may well fail*. For that reason, many of us have difficulty with this strategy. We recoil at the idea of making mistakes. This impulse is strengthened by the education system, which teaches us pretty much from the first day of school that there's a "right" and a "wrong" way to do something. The teachers hold the knowledge and ask the questions, and you answer them and are

---

*Trial and error might sound like just artlessly fiddling around, but the term refers to a recognized scientific research method developed by American psychologist Edward Lee Thorndike.

either "right" or "wrong." If you're often right, you're smart, and if you're often wrong, then you're stupid. From the moment that we're taught to think that way, we're constantly looking for the right answer. We're not allowed to discover; the notion that we might be able to arrive at new insights and uncover new opportunities is not fostered. If we're only answering questions that others ask us and learn by heart what others have discovered, how do we exercise our creativity? How do we find answers when there are no answers? To do that we need to make "mistakes." Lots of mistakes. Research shows that creative people make far more mistakes than less creative people do. Of course, how can we find new paths if we never get lost? If you're not failing occasionally, it's a sign you're stuck in old habits and not trying anything new or innovative.

To make the most of this strategy, we need open-mindedness, not only about possible solutions, but about what your goal is. This is the difference between seeking and finding. When you seek something, you already know what you're after. You've lost your keys, and it's them you must find to drive to work. You search for them until you find them. Done. But finding something novel calls for being unsure of your desired outcome. "When you go searching," psychologist Edel Maex says, "it means that you have a more or less defined idea of what you're looking for. Everything that you encounter on your path is compared to that image and pushed aside as soon as it doesn't fit that image. It's a process of selection and narrowing down. It's a great strategy for finding something again, but when using this method you'll never discover anything new."[1]

Only by consciously tinkering and being open to the unexpected can we come up with things that we couldn't have thought of beforehand. In the words of psychotherapist Steve de Shazer, "We never know what question we asked before we hear the answer."[2] There's a great word for this phenomenon—serendipity. Dutch serendipity researcher and Ig Nobel Prize winner (for improbable research that first makes people laugh and then makes them think) Pek van Andel has described serendipity as being like looking for a needle in a haystack and tumbling out with a farmer's daughter.

Even long-established companies sometimes simply tinker. Business success often involves a "logical explanation" cobbled together after the fact. Good luck or coincidence aren't often mentioned in management literature. We prefer logical theories, principles, or systems that give us the illusion that we know how to achieve success.

In truth, companies often lurch from one failure to the next, with just enough success in between. Intelligent companies acknowledge this and therefore constantly try new products or lines of business so they have a high enough quotient of successes. Their experimentation allows them constantly to learn and therefore grow and adapt. They're antifragile; able to rebound from setbacks. They often have a history of downturn followed by resurgence, and of many major changes in the nature of their business. Nokia, for example, was founded by Fredrik Idestam back in 1865 as a wood pulp mill. Later on, the company made rubber products such as tires and boots. From 1998 to 2012 Nokia was the world leader in the mobile phone market. It sold its billionth phone in Nigeria in the summer of 2005. But even such a dexterous shape-shifter can be suddenly disrupted by competitors. Once the iPhone came on the scene, Nokia was pushed from the world stage in less than two years. Microsoft acquired what was left of the company in 2013. Antifragility is no guarantee of eternal survival.

Mistakes, or accidental discoveries, have led to many famous innovations. Alexander Fleming discovered penicillin by pure coincidence. While he was tidying up his laboratory, he noticed that his Petri dishes of *Staphylococcus aureus* colonies had been contaminated by a mold, and there was a zone around that mold in which the bacteria didn't grow. He later analyzed the substance produced by the mold, which turned out to be penicillin. Then there's the story of George Crum, who worked as a cook in Saratoga Springs, New York. A customer complained that the potato slices he was served were far too thick. Just for fun, to tweak the customer, Crum cut extremely thin slices of potato and threw them into the deep fryer, so the potato chip was born.

Another stroke of luck, also in New York state, led Mary Phelps Jacob to a bountiful discovery. She was dressing for a debutante ball one evening in a corset that pinched terribly, and the points of the whalebones used to stiffen it poked out of her dress. She fashioned two silk handkerchiefs and a pink ribbon into an alternative corset, which proved to be the birth of the bra. In 1913 Mary filed a patent and founded the Caresse Crosby company. It was a great success. The Warner Brothers Corset Company offered her $1,500 for the patent. Mary was more than happy and accepted what was, for that time, a very impressive offer. Warner was happy too. The company made more than $15 million with the patent over the next 30 years.

Blotting paper was "discovered" when a papermaker accidentally forgot to add glue to paper pulp. The result was an extremely thin and absorbent paper. Viagra, LSD, the microwave, artificial sweeteners, brandy, and vulcanized rubber were also discovered by chance. Tinkering is an essential part of our culture, of our history of creation and innovation. There is virtually no groundbreaking innovation for which the original inventors imagined exactly how their breakthrough would ultimately be used. The transistor was originally developed for a limited number of military applications, but it turned out to have revolutionary consequences for the electronics industry. Diesel engines were originally thought to be suited only to trains. Photocopying was intended for specialized lithography applications. The idea of copying documents on a large scale—let alone the whole concept of the photocopier—played no role in its creation. The most disruptive innovation of our time, the internet, was created out of a series of inventions that enabled computers to share information with each other. Not even in their wildest dreams could those who came up with these individual technologies have imagined the extent to which the internet would change the world.

The late American sociologist James March, best known for his research into the behavior of organizations, argued that we need to "supplement the technology of reason with a technology of foolishness. Individuals and organizations need ways of doing things for which they have no good reason. Not always. Not usually. But sometimes. They need to act before they think."[3]

The ability to continue steadily on, always looking for new ways to do things, and not giving up due to failures, is perhaps the most important prerequisite of success. That might sound obvious, but it most certainly isn't. If you ask people what the best predictor of success is, many of them will say it's intelligence. Yet extensive research on the relationship between intelligence and success has shown that intelligence is only a fairly moderate predictor of success. There's a much stronger correlation with a completely different talent, one that's highly relevant to the strategy of persevering.

You may already be familiar with the famous experiment of the 1960s, carried out by psychologist Walter Mischel, where four-year-old children were left alone with marshmallows for an extended period of time. What was their task? "You can eat the marshmallow right away if you want to, but if you wait until the researcher comes back then you'll get another one as well." The researchers then secretly observed the children, counting the number of minutes each child was able to resist the impulse to eat the marshmallow. The children varied significantly. Some gobbled down the marshmallow just about as soon as the researcher had closed the door. Others did everything—but everything—to stop themselves from eating the marshmallow; they sat on their hands, bit their lips, looked away from the treat, sang songs, or rocked on their chairs. Some children managed to avoid eating the marshmallow for the entire 20-minute period the researcher was away.

The real beauty of the marshmallow experiment is that it was longitudinal: exactly the same group of children took part in follow-up research many years later. The findings? The four-year-olds who had resisted the temptation to eat the marshmallow the longest proved to be more successful in many aspects of life. They achieved higher marks at school, were more likely to complete a course of study, reported more stable relationships, had better self-esteem, better jobs, and were less susceptible to addiction. The talent they had demonstrated as children was delaying gratification in order to achieve a goal more valuable to use on the long run.[4] Delaying gratification is a powerful enabler of perseverance as our efforts to solve a problem fail.

A good example I came across was the story of an employee for the American company 3M who, come hell or high water, wanted to find a use for the waste from a sandpaper factory. He was convinced that there was an opportunity to be found. As he focused increasingly on finding a solution, he started neglecting his assigned work, and after a series of warnings he was fired. What did he do? He kept coming to work as if nothing had happened! Once this was noticed, he was denied access to the factory premises. As determined as he was, he continued his work in his attic at home. He stole the materials required for his experiments from his former employer. Finally, after years of failure, he managed to find an application for the waste materials; they could be made into a roofing product. The company even took him on again, and the Roofing Granules Division was set up under his management, which quickly proved to be extremely profitable. Fifteen years ago he retired a wealthy man.

The trick with this strategy of persevering is to keep *doing* things, looking for opportunities hiding within mistakes, opening yourself up to the totally unexpected. "Opportunity is missed by most people because it is dressed in overalls and looks like work," Edison said. The strategy of persevering is about getting back on your feet when you fall, brushing off the dust, and continuing. Consider how Albert Einstein explained his success: "If you ask someone to find a needle in a haystack, the average person will stop searching once they find it. I keep looking to see if there are other needles."

The strategy of focusing

Obstacles are things a person sees when
he takes his eyes off his goal.
—E. Joseph Cossman

Imagine that you want to open a bottle of wine to pour yourself a drink, but you can't get the cork out. You could spend ages trying to pry it out, but you could also just push the cork in. The aim is not "to get the cork out of the bottle" but "to drink the wine."

Both in everyday life and when faced with Important Things, we tend to lose sight of our goal. We get the goal and the means mixed up, focus on what we don't want (rather than on what we do want), or simply don't have a very clear idea of what we're aiming for. The *strategy of focusing* makes use of the creative power released when we aim very specifically for what we want, the very thing we have in mind. The sharper our focus, the greater the creative force. It's similar to the process of water-jet cutting, which uses water under extremely high pressure and in an incredibly thin stream effortlessly and extremely accurately to cut through all sorts of materials like stone, granite, and steel.

The essence of the strategy of focusing sounds simple: determine your end goal. Define clearly, unavoidably, and very precisely what you, in the end, really want and, after doing so, keep that goal in mind all the time. This can be far more difficult in practice than it at first sounds. In order to properly apply the strategy of focusing, it's important to distinguish between the goal and the means. As long as we focus on the means rather than on the goal—such as getting the cork out of the bottle rather than drinking the wine—our approach will tend toward stuck thinking. But, if we aim for the goal, for exactly what we want to achieve, then an apparently unsolvable problem can sometimes be flip-thought fairly easily. For example, there's a well-told story about then–Columbia University president Dwight Eisenhower, who later became the president of the United States, noticing that students tended to make their own paths across campus rather than using the established ones. These informal routes where the grass was worn away, so-called "elephant paths" or "desire paths," were unsightly. What did Eisenhower do? He shifted the focus. He realized the goal wasn't to get students to use the paved paths, it was to do away with unsightly paths. So he had the elephant paths made into nice, neat, paved ones.[1] (Unfortunately I have to admit I recently discovered this story about Eisenhower is not true at all. It's a tenacious myth that has been told over and over again. But, as it was literally too good to be true, I decided to keep it in the book. Better to be inspired by a good myth than to be demoralized by wretched reality.)

In the words of St. Thomas Aquinas, "If the highest aim of a captain were to preserve his ship, he would keep it in port forever." By asking ourselves again and again what exactly we have in mind, what we actually want, we can break through many deadlocks. Speaker and author Jos Burgers has a very helpful saying about this. "People don't want to buy a drill, they want to buy a hole."

In his book *Whatever You Think, Think the Opposite*, Paul

Arden relates the story of a Victorian literature professor relaxing naked on a riverbank. A nudist *avant la lettre*. Now in that era, exposure of any body part other than the head and hands was shameful. The professor saw a few of his students heading in his direction. They were going to spot him in a moment; it was unavoidable. He had nowhere to hide, and he only had a towel with him. There was no way that it would cover his whole body. He had only a fraction of a second to react. What could he do? Well, what did he want to achieve? On first thought you might say that his goal was not to be seen naked. But if you give it a bit more thought, it would be more accurate to say that his goal was not to be recognized by the students. So what did he do? With clear focus on his goal, he held the towel over his face.[2]

Psychologist and author Edward de Bono, who coined the term lateral thinking, writes about an island that is connected to the mainland by a bridge, with a toll levied in both directions. Only after 50 years did someone realize that just one tollbooth was necessary for crossing on to the island, because every car that arrived on the island at some point drove off it again. Monitoring cars coming and going wasn't the goal, making a certain amount of money was, and more money could be made without the expense of a second collection booth.

The examples above are fairly simple. Sometimes the goal and the means are more difficult to distinguish. During the Second World War, bomber planes returning from flights over Germany were analyzed by the US military to determine the number of bullet holes in each part of the aircraft. The military wanted to figure out how it could optimally reinforce planes with more armor to prevent them from being shot down, by putting more armor in the areas that got hit most. They asked the brilliant statistician Abraham Wald to examine the data, and he flip-thought the problem. He said that, in fact, the extra reinforcement should go on the places with the fewest bullet holes.

What the engineers hadn't factored in was that they didn't get to see all of the aircraft that made runs. They only saw planes that *hadn't* crashed. Wald understood that if a plane could make it back with a relatively high number of hits to some areas, such as the fuselage, then those places weren't the most critical. If very few planes returned with more than one or two hits to an area, then just a hit or two there seemed sufficient to down a plane. The area with the least holes in the returned planes was the engine, and Wald suggested that the extra armor should be concentrated there. The military took his advice, and from then on, the aircraft were fitted with extra plates on the undamaged places. Wald's intelligent suggestion—to focus on the places where there were no bullet holes—meant that from then on, many more bombers returned safely.[3]

When we look at the world around us, we can see that many problems have been flip-thought by redefining the goal and the means. Until fairly recently, businesses generally thought that all employees needed their own dedicated workstations. But this meant that often some stations were being unused some of the time, such as when people went on vacation or were sick, while there might at the same time be a shortage of workstations due to space limitations and expense. The problem was flip-thought by shifting the goal from "everyone has to have their own workstation" to "everyone who comes to work must have their own workstation." The change is subtle, but important. Once the goal was redefined in this way, it was only a small step to the practice known as hotdesking. Employees have a personal cabinet that they can roll to any workstation that's free. Hotdesking can deliver space savings of almost 50 percent, and around a 25 percent saving on office costs each year.

In order to make good use of the strategy of focusing, it's not only important to know how to formulate a goal properly—you also need to look at how *not* to do it. So where do we tend to go wrong when it comes to formulating our goals?

As we saw earlier, a first mistake is that we tend to formulate a goal *negatively*. Say you're not sure where you want to go for a vacation, so you consult a travel agent. The agent asks you where you want to go and you reply, "Well, I know I *don't* want to go to Spain. I had such a terrible time there." That answer is obviously of little help.

Focusing on what we don't want can sometimes ironically lead us to get exactly that. If you want to get to sleep, but you focus on not having insomnia, you likely won't be able to fall asleep. Focusing only on the negative aspects of a problem often leads to missed opportunities. Think about how to fight a big forest fire. It can sometimes be put out by setting another part of the forest on fire—obviously under very controlled circumstances—which creates an area of land without trees. When the fire reaches this area, it's unable to spread further.

In her book *The Glass Half-Full*, psychologist Suzanne C. Segerstrom writes about a man who was scared of the sound of sirens. Rather than focusing on avoiding the sound, he was challenged to study sirens, for example by buying toy ambulances with sirens for his daughter and considering whether the toys accurately reproduced the real sound, which meant he had to listen to real ones.[4]

There's a similar treatment for nightmares. Sufferers are challenged to reconstruct their nightmares during the day, as accurately as they can. Some Buddhists know this approach as "putting your head in the demon's mouth," after the Tibetan tale of Milarepa. Metaphorically if you are confronted with a fire-breathing dragon and try to flee it, the dragon is only going to spew more fire in your direction. But if you dare to put your head in its mouth, you'll see that there is really no dragon at all. The problem is only in your head.

A second mistake we often make when it comes to formulating our goals is to define them in vague ways. Two sisters were fighting over an orange. There was only one, and they both wanted it. All they could come up with was cutting it in two and each taking half. If only they had defined what they wanted in more precise terms, there wouldn't have been a dilemma. One of them wanted to drink the juice, the other wanted to grate up the peel for a cake.

We also tend to formulate our goals too grandly. "Someday" we'll travel the world. Or we'll write an autobiography "sometime." As long as we don't pick a first destination or set a deadline for finishing our tome, we're likely never to get started. Often with such grandiose goals, they're really more of a deflection from thinking about some underlying issue. The wish to take a trip around the world might well be based on the hope of escaping the daily grind. The idea of writing an autobiography might reflect a fear of departing this earth anonymous and unimportant.

A third mistake in defining goals is that we often fail to make a clear choice. We bet on two horses at once. Strangely enough, football teams can run into this problem when they score and find themselves in the lead. What's the new goal? Increase their advantage by focusing on more offensive gains or defend the lead?

A fourth mistake is that we set goals in areas in which we have no direct influence. Wanting to strive for happiness is understandable—but how do you do that? Emotions are flighty things. It's hard to order them up by command. Even more than that, striving to achieve a particular emotion may well have exactly the opposite effect. Psychology researcher J.W. Schooler conducted a study into the effect of pursuing happiness that showed doing so is counterproductive. In the experiment, different groups of research subjects listened to Stravinsky's *The Rite of Spring*. The first group was told to just listen to the music, while the second group was told to let the music cheer them up. The result? The first group felt the happiest. The other group, which was told to feel happier, actually felt less happy.[5]

A fifth and final mistake is that we often pursue goals that we're not authentically driven to achieve; we're not intrinsically motivated by them. We tell ourselves that we want something, but deep down we know we actually don't. That's often because the goals are deemed impressive by society, or because we're encouraged to pursue them, such as by our parents. Becoming a pop star or professional athlete or prima ballerina seems fantastic, but those achievements involve a great deal of sacrifice; we've got plenty of good reasons not to want them. Achieving some of these highly touted goals can require near obsession, and can prevent us from pursuing other goals that are important to us, such as spending quality time with our family and friends.

So we need to define and choose our goals carefully if we want to use the focusing strategy effectively. But how? One approach that has gained momentum in organizations in recent years is S.M.A.R.T. goal setting, which defines goals that are Specific, Measurable, Acceptable, Realistic, and Time-bound. Another powerful technique is one of the better-known interventions in the psychological approach called "solution-focused working," which has its origins in psychotherapy, but is now increasingly used in business coaching, training, and education. This technique is known as the "miracle question," which was hit upon more or less coincidentally when a client replied to a question from therapist Insoo Kim Berg with, "Oh, that would take a miracle!" Insoo responded with a very logical follow-up question: "OK, good, let's say that a miracle did happen. What would that look like?" Considering the answer to this question in regard to whatever goal we're aiming for helps keep our focus on the positive.[6]

To make sure we've set goals that motivate us, one trick is, strangely enough, to make sure they're somewhat overly ambitious. Goals that are set too low result in boredom and apathy. Goals set somewhat too high result in flow, the psychological state in which we are totally engaged with an endeavor. If you dare to make your goals so big that you realize that you can't achieve them unless you really go for it, you will astonish yourself with what you can accomplish. Ever since I learned this I've been instinctively setting absurdly high goals for myself. Two chapters today. Finish my to-do list by 12 o'clock. No, by 10 o'clock. I've discovered that by setting my goals almost twice as high as what I think is possible, I can put myself into such an attentive, energetic state that I can almost always achieve the goal.

To close, here's one final example. About reshuffling the means to an end.

The Ford Motor Company's suppliers packed their parts, such as carburetors, bumpers, and windshield wipers, in all sorts of different types of wooden formwork. On delivery, Ford employees took the parts out and threw the wooden formwork away. "It's a waste," Henry Ford decreed. Disposing of the wood cost time and money, valuable raw materials were being wasted. So Ford ordered all his suppliers to make formworks that met his precise specifications, including not only the types of wood to be used, but the thickness and length of the planks. He then reused the wood for the floorboards of the Model T.

In my opinion the story of the Ford Motor Company clearly

illustrates the potential of the strategy of focusing. When you encounter a problem, let go of what you don't want. In this case, stop focusing on the task of getting rid of the apparently redundant wooden formworks. When faced with a problem, take a breath and take your time to focus on what you *do* want. In the case of the Ford Motor Company this is of course to create cars as cheaply and efficiently as possible. Their main goal. This is how they came up with the idea of using the formworks as car parts.

What worked for the Ford Motor Company could work for all of us. By not allowing the immediate problem to block our vision, but instead focusing on our ultimate goal and values, we can step back, look at the bigger picture, and discover unexpected new possibilities.

The strategy of rethinking

*If you stop searching, you may find
that you are already there.*

When we have a problem and are searching for a solution, we're strongly inclined to think the solution will be found in the future. (Hopefully not too far in the future.) Yet that doesn't always have to be the case; a solution might have existed for a long time, buried in the past. Maybe nobody could find an application for it back then, until someone found a problem.

Quite a few discoveries and inventions that we think of as fairly recent actually have a long history but fell into obscurity for years. The ancient Greeks had figured out that the earth was round way back about 240 BC. Eratosthenes even calculated the circumference of the earth to within 2 percent accuracy. But for centuries this knowledge was lost. According to the early Christian worldview, the earth was flat, with Hell below and Heaven above. On the edges of the earth stretched the oceans, and if you sailed too close to their edges, you might fall off. Indigenous peoples in Latin America invented the wheel long before it was put to world-changing use, but it was used as a children's toy. Similarly, the steam engine, the machine that drove the Industrial Revolution, was invented in primitive form 1,700 years previously by the Greek engineer and mathematician Hero of

Alexandria, but the device was used only as a toy. The escalator as we know it today was also initially just an amusement. In 1897, Charles Seeberger developed a fairground attraction called "Stairway to Hell," and a number of years would pass before someone thought of using this discovery to move people from one floor to another.

As an aside, it's interesting to note that quite a few ground-breaking inventions were originally created for entertainment. Perhaps we're more creative when we're able to play than when we are at work? But back to the main point . . .

Imagine how many patents might be languishing unused in the registries of the various authorities around the world? But the fact that inventions disappear into obscurity is not my key message here. What I want to emphasize is that we humans often invent brilliant things without the faintest idea of how they might actually be useful. We have gold in our hands but we don't even know it. With the *strategy of rethinking* we take another look at our situation and resources, and search for hidden possibilities. Sometimes we have a possibility right in front of us, it's just that we don't recognize it as such. Sometimes the possibility of the moment is so precisely identical to the problem of the moment that you simply can't see it. You are in the middle of a possibility, but you think you're in the middle of a problem. It's day, but you think that it's night.

Maybe, at this point, you're wondering what the difference is between the strategy of perseverance and the strategy of rethinking. In a way they might look alike. But there's an important difference. In the case of perseverance you start where you are and, by working your way through, you might stumble upon an unexpected opportunity. Rethinking works the other way around. You start with a possibility and by examining reality you might stumble upon a problem that can immediately be flipped by a possibility that's already there.

A Beagle Boys cartoon illustrated this point cleverly. A Disney creation, the Beagle Boys were a gang of criminals, and in this story, they are in prison. It's their day of release and they're in a fantastic mood, dreaming about the future. Their fantasies run wild. They'll live in a huge castle with thick walls and a lovely courtyard, and staff will serve them their meals. The result? When it comes time for their release, they don't want to leave. Of course, prisons are really nothing like lavish castles, but you get the point.

A great real-life case of this is that of 3M Company researcher Spencer Silver. In the late 1960s, Silver was trying to come up with a better glue for adhesive tape. It needed to be extra-strong, but the glue Silver created was the exact opposite. He accidentally came up with a super-weak glue, which hardened very, very slowly. What a problem. Well, no, what a possibility without a problem, yet. It took five years before a problem Silver's glue could solve was discovered. His colleague Arthur Fry, annoyed by the way his bookmark kept constantly falling out of his hymnbook while he was singing at church, suddenly recalled Spencer Silver's glue and, with his own moment of inspiration, the Post-it Note was born. Post-its are now viewed as the most important innovation in office supplies since the paperclip. Silver and Fry received 3M's most prestigious award for their groundbreaking work.

Another failed product that was full of possibility became Silly Putty, The Wonder Toy of the Twentieth Century. It was created in the 1940s by James Wright, a researcher at General Electric. He was trying to create a synthetic substitute for rubber, for use in the war. The stretchy substance was of no interest to the military, but toy-store owner Ruth Fallgatter heard about it and all sorts of things it could do. You could throw it at a window and it would stick; you could roll it over a newspaper and it would make a copy of the print. What fun! She recommended to businessman Peter Hodgson that it might make a great toy, and just before Easter of 1950, Silly Putty, packed in plastic eggs, hit the shelves. It became so popular that in 1968 there was even a rumor that the Apollo 8 crew had taken it to the moon to hold their tools in place. When Hodgson died in 1976, his personal fortune was estimated at $140 million.

The rethinking strategy requires optimism. You have to believe that possibilities are often hiding in plain sight and keep your eyes peeled for them. An astounding study by psychologist Richard Wiseman showed the blinding effects of pessimism. His research subjects were divided into two groups: one of people who considered themselves lucky, and the other of people who considered themselves unlucky. Wiseman sent all of the subjects to a restaurant, where he had placed a £10 note on the floor in the doorway. Almost none of the "unlucky" participants saw the £10 note, and almost all of the "lucky" group did. Pessimistic people tend to focus more on the problem than the prospect.[1]

To help keep your eyes peeled for prospects, let me introduce the concept of "drifting possibility"; that there are possibilities all around us, as though they're drifting about, but we're not seeing them. We've got to actively look for them. Often, we'll discover they've been right in front of us for some time.

The Dutch automobile manufacturer DAF made such a discovery concerning the diesel car engines they were running tests on in their factories. For years, it hadn't occurred to anyone that that the engines could actually be used to do something while they were tested. Finally, someone thought: hang on, if they have to run anyway, why don't we use them to generate electricity? The engines turned out to generate enough power to light an entire factory complex.

As we've seen, identifying possibilities is often about spotting unexpected applications for some item or creation you already have. Well, we can also create opportunities by convincing people of an application they haven't thought they needed. This is what I'll call the "infomercial technique," used by TV shopping channels. They specialize in advertising products that nobody actually *needs*, like a super-duper back scratcher. The ads usually begin with rhetorical questions like, "Do you, too, suffer from an itchy back you just can't scratch?" Cut to footage of people with really itchy backs, trying awkwardly to scratch them with inferior back scratchers from other manufacturers. One causes cuts and slight scabbing, which leads to even more itching. Another is so badly made that it breaks while a woman is using it, hurting her back. Throw those horrible back scratchers away, we're told, and we see shots of scratchers being tossed in garbage cans with a big red X over the screen. There's a better way: the one and only Happy Back Scratcher. Perky music plays. We see a content gentleman using the Happy Back Scratcher while on the phone. Then a shot of a whole family delightedly scratching their backs, not only in the living room watching TV, but on vacation, and even while exercising. The kids are doing better at school and the parents at work, and they even live three years longer on average! But that's still not all—today, with your order, you'll receive a Happy Head Scratcher as well!

This example of the Happy Back Scratcher, of course, is a little bit absurd, but ask yourself this: what are the possibilities and qualities of whatever I have at my disposal at this point of my life, and how can I use them to flip my problem or solve the problems of others? If you have a car and other people don't, for them your car is an opportunity. If you are the owner of a deserted factory, for an organizer of a rave party this could be the perfect location. When you don't have a job, of course that's a real problem. But what do you have? Lots of time. See this time not as a problem to be solved, but as a possibility to be realized. Maybe it's time finally to take a tour around the world, start your own business, or have a sabbatical. Wherever you are, whatever you possess, approach your reality as a possibility and consider opportunities you might have overlooked.

In human history, there has never been a better period than now in which to apply the rethinking strategy. The internet has made this the most opportunistic time ever. Obviously, everyone agrees that the internet has changed, and continues to change, our lives radically. The potential it offers for rethinking can't be overestimated. Problems that seemed unsolvable in the past are now seen in a new light. Past problems like how to sell your collection of toy cars or how to find a romantic partner, given that you live in a village with a population of 2,000, have been flip-thought as opportunities thanks to the internet.

The strategy of rethinking can also be used in another way, not by rewinding but by fast-forwarding through time. One of the wonderful things about being human is that we are able not only to reassess the past, but to use our imagination of the future to assess the present. When I had just started working for myself—I was about 35—and often wondered whether resigning from my job had been the right decision, I regularly had an imaginary conversation with myself. Well, actually between my 35-year-old self, on my left, and my 70-year-old self, on my right. The 35-year-old would ask, for example, "Will I be able to earn enough money to support my family?" and the 70-year-old would reply with something like, "I understand that you're worried about money now but let that go and focus on what you're good at, what gives you energy." These dialogues always reassured me, as if I really did have a 70-year-old deep within me, who had more confidence in me than my 35-year-old self.

Rethinking by imagining the future can also be used effectively in conversations with others. A few years ago I encountered a remarkable story about a serious conflict between a school's deputy headmaster and one of the students. The student had gotten into a fight with the school's caretaker, and the deputy head felt that the student should apologize. However, the student refused to do so. He believed that the caretaker had treated him unfairly. The student adviser was asked to step in, and he asked the student which year he was in. The student was going to graduate soon. The adviser then asked the boy where he thought he'd be in another two years. The student answered that he would be at college in Rotterdam. So the adviser asked him if, when he was studying in Rotterdam, he would run into a problem like this. The student burst out laughing. No way—he'd be past this sort of thing. Finally, the adviser asked the student whether his future self might be able to give his present self some tips for handling the problem. What did the student do? He started to recite what the deputy head had told him he should do. He rethought the situation from the perspective of his wiser, older self.

Here's one final bit of rethinking magic for your entertainment.

Alongside his work as a theater and television producer, the Belgian artist Kamagurka is a successful cartoonist and painter. Despite his success in art, he considers himself only moderately gifted, particularly when it comes to producing good likenesses in a portrait. But Kamagurka saw a possibility in this shortcoming. He started a new trend in art: accidentalism. Kamagurka paints portraits wildly and randomly, without a subject in mind, and uploads them to the internet. The public can then nominate people whom they think look like the portrait. The person who most resembles the portrait is then designated the subject.

Wherever you are, whatever you do, whatever skills or talents you possess, keep revisiting and rethinking ideas or opportunities you might have overlooked. See them all as a potential solution. For what? No idea. You just don't know! Is that a problem? No! Not knowing is exactly the essence of the strategy of rethinking. So start with these possibilities and then work your way back to see how they might solve existing problems, or problems you hadn't even realized existed. Your problems or those of others. The nice thing is to think of how many answers to our problems might already be out there, waiting to be spotted.

Battle

Strategies 8 to 11

The strategy of eliminating

The strategy of importing

The strategy of collaborating

The strategy of enticing

These strategies are to be used when the reality is hostile to us. Dishonesty, manipulation, and greed are real human characteristics that we have to deal with. Key elements of these strategies are management, temptation, persuasion, and collaboration.

The strategy of eliminating

Endings can be opportunities for new beginnings.

Some people consider flip thinking to be a kind of positive-thinking-happy-hippie movement. A sort of paradise, an Aladdin's cave of thinking in opportunities and possibilities; as if flip thinking was 100 percent synonymous with optimism and positivity. Well, that's not the case. Flip thinking is not one single discipline, theory, or approach; its strategies are just as varied, changeable, and versatile as life itself. So it is that the *strategy of eliminating* is based on the understanding that mourning, loss, and pain are inevitable. Recognizing this fact forms the basis of this strategy.

In February 2008 Polaroid announced that it was to close its factories in Massachusetts, Enschede in the Netherlands, and in Mexico. Polaroid's film and cameras were displaced by digital cameras; it had already filed for bankruptcy in 2001, and its new owners declared bankruptcy again in 2008. Just a little more than 70 years after the Polaroid Corporation was founded in 1937, the curtain fell for the company, although the brand name is still used by yet another owner.

Polaroid is one of many once-thriving brands that have ceased to exist in their original form, and companies' life spans are getting shorter and shorter. Nowadays the rise and fall of an entire sector may take fewer than 15 years. The first *Forbes* Top 100, the list of the biggest companies in the United States, dates back to 1917. Seventy years later, in 1987, 61 of those 100 companies had disappeared. Of the remaining 39, only 18 were still in the Top 100. So were those 18 doing well? No. Over that 70-year period, they performed on average at least 20 percent worse than the rest of the market. Only two of the companies, General Electric (GE) and Kodak, performed better than the market average, and since then Kodak has spent a period in bankruptcy too. Think about it: just one company that was listed in the *Forbes* Top 100 in 1917 is still in existence and performing better than the average. The other 99 companies have disappeared or are performing worse than average. What lesson can we learn from this? Simple. It's not only a harsh reality or an unlucky circumstance that can change our fortune, it's even worse, in the end everything disappears. As we have seen before this is a sad, but unavoidable reality. Nothing lasts forever. We can see this fact as a problem, but we can also see it as an opportunity. That's exactly what the strategy of eliminating does. Often the ending of one opportunity can lead to the birth of another.

The world is changing at breakneck speed, and companies everywhere are facing a vexing question: modernize, adapt, or close down? In the first Dutch edition of this book, published in 2008, I wrote,

> How will the music industry respond to music downloading? In the Netherlands, sales of CD singles stopped this year. With a simple click of the mouse, you can download *Rolling Stone's 500 Greatest Songs of All Time* in one go, with all the songs neatly labelled. Then you import them into your computer, sync them with your iPod, and later on you can listen to them on the go. It all

sounds so modern, but someone reading this in five years'
time will think it's a pathetic little story.

Well, we're now more than another ten years down the line and
that passage does indeed sound pathetic. Who downloads? You
put your phone in the holder in your car, start up Spotify, and
stream. Which sounds so current, but how will we view it when
we look back on it in another five or ten years? What will we be
able to do by then?

You might be asking yourself why this chapter starts with a
long discussion of the fact that things change, that what cur-
rently exists constantly threatens to vanish and new things are
constantly coming on to the scene. That's obvious. What's the
point? Well, regarding flip thinking, the point is that we can
benefit from this change. How? By completely letting go of
what no longer works, or soon won't work anymore. Only by
constantly and rigorously daring to stop doing what's no longer
working are we able to make room for what might actually
work. So the strategy of eliminating also starts with identifying
what's not working. To really be able to apply this strategy, you
have to be able to prune, metaphorically cutting back the dead
wood from the tree. Which is not always easy. It often involves
pain and mourning.

Take the case of General Electric (GE). Its success is largely
attributed to its practice of self-destruction. Under the leadership of long-time CEO Jack Welch, GE adopted a strategy of
eliminating operations that were not sufficiently successful, setting a high standard for success. The motto Welch introduced
was: either we're at the top of a market segment, or we pull out.
He also instituted a strict policy of letting go of the lowest-
performing 10 percent of employees.[1]

The strategy of eliminating comes in many shapes and sizes.

Let's start with the most obvious version: *if something is going to stop working in the near future, stop doing it.* If a product or service will shortly cease to exist, stop offering it right away, even if it seems at the core of who you are or what you do.

The strategy of eliminating works not only because you stop doing what's not working, but because cutting back the dead wood leaves you with a healthy tree. In eliminating what's of no value, you can focus on the value of what's left. So eliminating isn't just about throwing away—it's also about retaining. It's a strategy that both destroys *and* preserves.

At the height of the 2008 credit crunch, the financial services firm ING ran into major problems, as did so many. The organization held an impressive staff party every year, but with the economic trouble, holding a lavish party was inappropriate. That didn't mean there would be no party at all. Some of the ING staff were talented singers and cooks, and a group of employees voluntarily took charge of organizing a low-budget affair, which was such a resounding success that it was repeated the next year.[2]

The strategy of eliminating is actually similar to that of amplifying. The difference lies chiefly in the order of the process: with amplifying you start with what's good and look at what you can do with it, while with eliminating you start with what's not working and then you look at what's left. Let's say that you want to rid your lawn of weeds. You can either remove the weeds (eliminating), or you can feed the grass so that it grows stronger and chokes out the weeds (amplifying). You will need to use your intuition to decide which strategy to choose in a particular situation. Is the problem mostly that something's clearly going wrong? Then start by eliminating. If it's not clear what's not working, then start by focusing instead on what's working and amplifying.

The second version of eliminating pays heed to the wisdom of the saying, "Insanity is doing the same thing over and over and expecting a different result." We so often just keep trying harder and harder with an approach that's not working. The second variant of eliminating says: *stop doing things that don't work*. Just stop. Often this creates a new opportunity.

To the annoyance of the management, an IT company was constantly losing its new staff. The company was following all the conventional wisdom about hiring and retention. The firm's recruitment process was elaborate and expensive, and it put new employees through an excellent training program. It also tried raising salaries, but that also didn't work. Many new staff members had barely completed the training before they were poached by the competition. Finally, the management decided to say "yes-and" to the situation. They eliminated the idea that they should be retaining all these brilliantly trained employees, and set up a subsidiary that provides training and education for people who want to fast-track their careers. After all, they'd discovered they were good at it! The solution was a win–win. It made the firm more attractive to high-potential young employees, who figured it "got" them, and also earned lots of money! So much, in fact, that it became the firm's core business. The company moved away from a great deal of its IT service work and became a successful training firm.[3]

Stopping what's not working can have the most surprising effects. New York City's subway stations have for years been treated like trash cans, with passengers throwing all sorts of litter on the platforms and tracks. So what did the authorities do? They placed more and more trash cans on the platforms. Did it work? No. On the contrary, the amount of litter only seemed to increase. So the Metropolitan Transportation Authority (MTA) carried out a test, removing all the trash cans from two stations.

This resulted in 50 percent to 67 percent less litter. An MTA representative concluded that: "If there is nowhere to discard trash, riders will take it with them—often outside of a station." Perhaps trash cans were even sending a message that it's absolutely fine to litter because it will be cleaned up.[4] The test was since extended to other subway stations and public places.

So how can you apply this elimination strategy in your own life? Start by looking for the things that aren't working. If you're struggling to keep on top of your to-do lists, you might implement new systems, more notebooks, calendar reminders, etc. It's a common mistake that we think we have to do more in order to keep momentum going. That's why we end up with lots of unnecessary techniques, systems, and to-do lists. As mentioned, eliminating things that don't work is like chopping the dead wood off a tree. What you're left with is a living, healthy organism. Keep life simple. Try to do (a lot) more by doing (a lot) less.

A third variant of eliminating is the *deconstructing* tactic. Choose something, take part of it away, and look into whether you can create something new with what you have left. What would a restaurant be like without chairs? Soccer with no ball? A television without a remote? A car without a steering wheel? Many inventions have been created this way. After all, isn't a mobile phone essentially a telephone without a cord?

For start-up companies, the cost of business premises is often a stumbling block. What if you were to just do without premises? I came across an innovative day-care company that picks the children up from school in a bus and takes them on trips, such as for a walk in the woods, or a visit to a farm to watch the birthing of lambs in spring, ice skating or sledding in winter, swimming in summer, and raking leaves in fall. Now they have five flourishing projects in four cities. Not because they have a building, but because they don't have a building at all. The elimination of something that was holding them back (the cost of renting or buying a premises) became their unique selling point.

Want to hold shorter meetings? Try eliminating chairs. Dutch company TNO decided to experiment with this. It's far less comfortable to stand during a meeting, and sure enough, this led to more efficiency. In fact, TNO found that these so-called "stand-up meetings" were a third shorter. As meetings in the Netherlands have been estimated to cost 30 billion euros per year, stand-up meetings nationwide could potentially lead to 10 billion euros in savings.[5]

A fourth variant of this strategy is *eliminating an assumption*. Does something always have to be done in a certain way? What you do with this variant is challenge your ingrained ideas of how things "should be." A produce seller at the farmers' market was doing well, on the whole, with good sales and sufficient profit. The problem was that he had to work like crazy. He should really have taken on another two or three people to help him, but their wages and benefits would be too expensive and he didn't want to pay people off the books. What could he do? Pay half on the books and half off? Recruit volunteers? He fretted himself silly until he gave up the whole idea of staff, rediscovering a concept that's been around for about 120 years in the food business—self-service. He constructed his stall with bins arranged in a U shape and had people serve themselves. All he had to do was ring up the sales.

"Every organization needs a leader" is a fundamental business maxim. Why? Who says? The Synergy School is a progressive private school in South Africa that emphasizes taking responsibility for oneself. The founder, owner, and driving force of the school—a guru in the eyes of a number of staff members—suddenly announced that he no longer wanted to be headmaster. Based on his fervent belief that "only by creating chaos do you release energy," he left the matter of how the school would thereafter be run open. In great haste, a team assembled to find a new headmaster, but it was quickly obvious that there was no suitable successor. After all, who could really replace the founder? But then the team had a great idea. Why not apply its philosophy of giving responsibility to the staff? Why did the school need a headmaster? It wasn't a legal requirement. The team decided to divide the headmaster's duties among the teachers, the rest of the staff, and the owners, and the school became a self-managing organization.[6]

Eliminating assumptions can lead to major breakthroughs. We assume trains should depart at fixed times. But what if we tried eliminating that assumption? What if trains just ran very often on some lines? Say every 15, 10 or, where possible, 5 minutes? In that case, people don't have to adjust their travel plans to fixed times, they can just arrive at the platform and take the next train. No matter what time it is. Wouldn't that—when possible—be a lot better for everybody than scheduled trains? Author Richard Bach eliminated the assumption that the book he'd written for children, *Jonathan Livingston Seagull*, had to be published as a children's book. No publisher was interested in it until he pitched it as a homily for adults too. The book became a worldwide bestseller.

What about your assumptions about your job? Australian Ron Mueck was working as a window dresser. He was very creative, and rather than use the typical stock figures, he started making his own models in the 1980s, which over time became striking hyperrealistic figures that incorporated real biological materials, such as chicken skin, blood vessels, and hair. When an art collector discovered his work, Mueck was elevated from modelmaker to artist.

Perhaps you have a job with a detailed job description and a résumé that can be considered as a sort of packaging for your talents and experience. What if you were to eliminate that packaging? What opportunity might that produce? Professor of innovation and consultant Jeff Gaspersz was working for a major consulting firm when he decided to go out on his own, starting his own consultancy. He writes:

> At a certain point in my career I felt it was stagnating. A friend said something to me for which I'm still grateful. She said, "Think in terms of energy. Your energy to achieve what you want is unstoppable. All it needs is another context in which it can keep on flowing." In a flash, that idea gave me a completely different view of my own situation. I suddenly realized that my creative energy isn't dependent on a specific place. That sudden change in my perspective felt like a tingling sensation, a sort of emotional liberation. That's what led me to start my own business.[7]

We tend to think that success comes from doing things, which is logical, but it's not the whole story. Success often also involves not doing things. How much of our time do we fill with the most inane matters? If we want to be truly successful, we need to start by stopping that. Clearing our schedules. Throwing all the nonsense overboard. Instead of to-do lists, we should start each day with a not-to-do list: what am I *not* going to do today in order to be successful? You can quickly dispense with obvious wastes of your time, like cleaning up other people's messes. But also consider things you're doing because you assume you have to in order to be seen positively by others, such as returning every phone call or email immediately. More than anything, success is about being able to *not* do things. In the words of Steve Jobs, "Focusing is about saying no."

Eliminating can be wonderfully freeing, but also painful. If you don't like gardening, you can have your whole garden paved over. If you no longer trust yourself to drive safely, you can get rid of your car. Not easy, but a great solution. Ending a relationship that's not working anymore. Ouch. Quitting your job. Cutting off contact with a relative. These are difficult types of eliminating but, however painful they are, they are also liberating—painful endings can be opportunities for new beginnings. Often it's better not to wait for elimination to happen to you and instead to take control into your own hands. There's a Dutch proverb: "Don't throw out your old shoes before you have new ones." Seems like great advice, but the strategy of eliminating begs to differ. Often continuing with an enterprise that's no longer working is much more painful than making the break. What have you got to lose? As a good friend of mine put it, "If you want to create something, start with emptiness: the stronger the vacuum, the greater the force of attraction."

So burn your boats. Your old shoes? Chuck them! Walk around for a while with bare feet, or how about flippers? Start that business. Or you want to be a landscape painter? Go rent a studio and pick up a brush. Want to travel? Get that trailer and head off toward the horizon. If you know deep inside that what you're doing isn't working, *stop*!

The strategy of importing

If you can't beat them, buy them.

In the Netherlands, the presentation of the annual national budget is on *Prinsjesdag,* the day of the king's speech, which is the third Tuesday in September. The Ministry of Finance informs the press of the budget only shortly before the big day, under strict embargo. But in 2004, leading broadcaster RTL News was able to get word of the budget almost a week early due to a leak. The following year the ministry imposed especially tight security, but RTL News again managed to get hold of the scoop early. So the ministry decided to change tack. Pieter Klein was employed as the ministry's new chief information officer. Where was he working before that? That's right. He was the political editor of RTL News. The approach worked. Due to his knowledge of how leaking works, the budget wasn't leaked that year and was announced as it should be, with great pride on the day of the king's speech.

You can fight your enemy or you can try to make him your ally. If you can't beat them, join them. Or, as in the ministry's case, buy them. The *strategy of importing* uses this insight; transform opponents from "them" into "we." Soccer clubs know this well and regularly sign the best players of key competitors. Two birds with one stone: you've obtained a good player and your opponent has lost one.

We can import "enemy forces" in a number of situations, rang-ing from friendly to life threatening. It just depends on what your relationship is with "the enemy." Say you're a teacher. You might have done some battle over students using mobile phones in class. Quite a lot of teachers are driven up the wall by it. Some schools even require students to put their mobile phones in a box at the front of the room when they come into class. Obviously this is an example of stuck thinking. It creates lots of student resentment. For this reason, more and more teachers are starting to have students use their phones as learning tools instead. After all, they're pocket-sized computers. Why not put all of that power to good use?!

Comedian Sara Kroos pulled off a similar example of a gentle form of importing the enemy. A Mardi Gras band was performing in the same building as she was, making so much noise that it was disrupting her performance. She invited the group to come and play for her audience. The band accepted the invitation, and to the great hilarity of the audience, the show was transformed into a raucous Mardi Gras party.

Hostile company takeovers are a somewhat more heavy-handed way of importing. Obviously the same strategic payoff of a soccer club signing another's star player is at play: taking over an enemy is an extremely efficient way of rendering him harmless. You get rid of a competitor and simultaneously acquire new talent and knowledge. But hostile takeovers aren't without risk. In by far most of the cases, the new company's profit after the takeover is even smaller than the combined profit of the two companies prior to the acquisition. But when it works, as was the case in Philips's successful takeover of the chip manufacturer VLSI in 1999, and the acquisition of German company Mannesmann by Vodafone a year later, then it's a "two birds with one stone" scenario.[1]

The basic strategy of importing can be applied broadly. When the city of Amsterdam wanted to ensure that a new model of subway cars would be vandal proof, alderman Mark van der Horst put forward an audacious proposal. Invite notorious vandals to come and demolish one of them; that would be the best way to learn how to thwart vandalism. Military organizations also often employ the strategy, such as by employing hackers to help beef up IT security, as well as by soliciting the assistance of spies as double agents. Police and the secret services frequently make use of the strategy too; use a thief to catch a thief.

The German village of Wunsiedel made brilliant use of this ploy. Every November, neo-Nazis march through the village, where Rudolf Hess, the second-in-command of the Third Reich, was buried, making Wunsiedel a place of pilgrimage for extreme right-wing demonstrators. The locals tried for years to stop the march, without success, and then in November 2014, they flip-thought the problem. The local business community turned the Nazi march into a sponsored walk: for every meter covered by the demonstrators, 10 euros would be donated to anti-Nazi organization EXIT-Germany. This meant that the Nazis were effectively demonstrating against themselves: the further they walked, the better. The neo-Nazis ultimately raised more than 10,000 euros for the anti-extremist organization.[2]

Adversaries don't have to be our enemies. This insight has led to the realization that businesses can turn critical, even angry, customers into advisers. Criticism, especially non-constructive criticism, might be taken as a form of hostility; we tend to consider criticism as a personal attack. But most often, people express their frustration or dissatisfaction because they want their needs met. All organizations can learn from listening to those needs. Smart businesses have developed processes for carefully considering customer complaints and using them to make improvements.

Some organizations take this a step further and actually solicit the participation of critics in their work. De Tussenvoorziening, a Dutch organization that provides shelter and support services to homeless people in the city of Utrecht, does this brilliantly. Founder and director Jules van Dam recounted to me that "the early years were the hardest." Some of the residents of neighborhoods where shelters were being created would angrily object. The organization learned to accept their resistance as an essential part of its work. As Van Dam says, "At the first meeting in a new neighborhood, there's always a huge fuss. Usually there are two or three people who try to get the community against us. But afterward there are always a couple of people who come over to us and are a bit ashamed of their fellow residents. They tell us they support our objectives but that they're also concerned. These are exactly the people that we'd like to have involved in the process."

The organization creates a management group for each new shelter, which is tasked with coordinating the whole process, and some of these people who are concerned but also supportive are asked to participate. This has helped the organization learn about improvements it can request the city to make in neighborhoods as a condition of creating the shelters, such as putting streetlights on a dark street. "Our goal is that the neighborhood will be improved thanks to our facility," says Van Dam. "We take complaints from the neighborhood seriously, and we make a note of them in a contract that we make with all parties involved." In time, the communities become receptive to the shelters, with some of the residents saying they're proud that their neighborhood is helping to get a facility off the ground. "I must add," says Van Dam, "that it only works if we, for our part, are always completely open and honest. About the difficult things, too."

After a facility has been running for a year, the organization has a party for it, and Van Dam says that usually one of the people who was really angry at first comes over to him and tells him something like, "You should have said to start with that it would all work so well!" One such objector had become so supportive that he offered to go to another neighborhood to champion a shelter. But it turned out not to go well. People thought he was a plant, not a real member of the community he was from. "Our supporter was bewildered," Van Dam recalled when I spoke to him. " 'Was I really that bad?' he asked me later on, and, I told him honestly, 'No, you were worse.' "

One of the most inspiring practitioners of the strategy of importing is Nelson Mandela. His whole life is convincing evidence of how one person can transform an entire society by experiencing the enemy as "one of us." Perhaps the best proof of this is this story about the Springboks, the South African rugby team. The Springboks were originally dominated by white Afrikaners, and were therefore despised by many Black South Africans during apartheid. The team's symbol, the springbok, which is a type of antelope, evoked strong anger, and immediately after the African National Congress (ANC) came to power in 1995 people called for the symbol to be banned. Mandela, as president, was under a lot of pressure to do so.

That year, after a long boycott, South Africa was once again able to take part in international rugby tournaments, and to the frenzied excitement of the entire country, across the racial divide, the Springboks made it to the final of the Rugby World Cup. The game was the match of the year. Just before kickoff, Mandela stepped onto the field to wish his fellow countrymen good luck. How did he do so? He literally imported the signs and symbols of the "enemy"; he was dressed in a green and gold Springboks shirt bearing the number of the captain, Francois

Pienaar. The whole stadium burst into wild chanting, "Nelson! Nelson!" Following the match, Mandela issued an official declaration that the Springboks would be allowed to keep their emblem. It was a powerful gesture of reconciliation. And the outcome of the match? South Africa won the final—what else?—and became world champions for the first time in history.

You might wonder how to apply the strategy of importing in daily life. Well, the first thing you can do when you encounter a potential enemy or competitor is ask yourself the question: what does he or she possess that I can use? What motives or qualities do they have that I could possibly incorporate that might support my goals? So, suppress your first instinct to see and dismiss the other as "the enemy," and to fight him or her, but investigate the other as a possible "part of you." Take the time to work out whether it might be possible to, like Nelson Mandela did, "wear their shirt."

Does your sister-in-law have a tendency to over-organize everything in life? Don't fight her. Incorporate her. Let her arrange your wedding! Does your uncle irritate you because he's always monologuing about his business success? Ask him to do the keynote speech at your next work event! Is your boss overcontrolling? Ask him to check in detail all essential parts of the project you're working on, and save yourself a bit of time and energy.

In essence, don't fight them, don't collaborate with them (that's for the next chapter), but incorporate them. Use them in your projects. Under your flag.

The strategy of collaborating

Do I not destroy my enemies when I make them my friends?
—Abraham Lincoln

Some boys at a school teased a younger boy by frequently asking him to choose between a nickel and a dime. To the malicious glee of the others, he always chose the nickel because it was "the bigger coin." The boy's teacher spoke to him and explained that a dime is worth more than a nickel. "I know," said the boy, "but once they know that I know, they'll stop giving me money."

When we face a (supposed) enemy, there's a good chance we'll become engaged in a power struggle. How does the power game work? It's simple. You make threats, force the other to give in, and if you have enough power, you'll have him on his knees. You get what you want. End of conflict. If the other party turns out to be stronger than you, then bad luck for you. But in both cases the conflict is resolved. This is the winner-takes-all model.

Unfortunately, conflicts are rarely resolved so cleanly. More often, a bitter and protracted struggle ensues. The worst instance of this is trench warfare. The more time, money, and energy both parties invest in the fight, the more difficult it is to give in. Both parties lose in the end. As the saying goes, "An eye for an eye makes the whole world blind." Wars, strikes, and divorce battles often follow this pattern. You end up willing to suffer many losses, out of fear that the other party will do better than you. Like an estranged partner who thinks, "I'm absolutely not going to quit the relationship, because I don't want them to be happier with someone new."

Even if you win the battle, you can still lose the war. In winning there's a good chance you have humiliated your opponent and anger over that will come back to you, like a boomerang. Why did the peace achieved at the end of the First World War not last? Because the German people felt they had been treated atrociously by the treaty that ended the war. Most often, the best guarantee for a definitive end to battle is not the other party's submission, but reaching a satisfactory agreement between both parties. As the British Prime Minister Benjamin Disraeli wrote, "Next to knowing when to seize an opportunity, the most important thing in life is to know when to forego an advantage."[1]

During the American Civil War, Abraham Lincoln gave a speech in which he characterized the rebels from the South in the most friendly terms. An elderly woman, an inveterate Unionist, was angry with Lincoln. There was a war on after all! Lincoln responded to her objection, "Do I not destroy my enemies when I make them my friends?"

What we can do with these hostile situations—turn a problem into an opportunity, turn a threat into a new opportunity—we can also do with people: we can make a pact with a (supposed) enemy, make him an ally. We can redirect the energy that has been turned against us into a common goal. That is the essence of the collaboration strategy. The differences are forgotten, the similarities emphasized.

The term collaboration is (unfortunately) a historically loaded term, especially in my native Netherlands, where it refers to the collaboration with the German occupier in the Second

World War and is therefore equivalent to treason. Yet I have deliberately chosen to keep this term for this strategy because it describes exactly what the intention is: to cooperate with the enemy.

The strategy of collaborating takes the energy that's being used against us and channels it toward a common goal. Differences are underplayed and similarities emphasized. The strategy can be employed not only with hostile opponents but with neutral—or even friendly—parties too. Enemies and apparent enemies come in all shapes and sizes. Therefore, several different approaches can be used within this strategy. You could say "sub-strategies."

Collaborating and importing might seem similar, but there is actually an important difference. With importing, the hostile party is brought into the fold, but with collaborating, they remain independent. You work as partners. There are many ways of going about this. One of the best is the win–win solution—something that ultimately benefits both parties.

In some parts of the world, it's easier to obtain Coca-Cola than it is to get hold of essential medicines. Too crazy for words, but that's the reality. Why not hitch a ride on the remarkably extensive distribution network of the world's biggest soft-drink brand? This was the thought behind the ColaLife initiative, which uses Coca-Cola's distribution system to transport anti-diarrhea packages to remote regions in Zambia. Across large parts of Africa, dehydration caused by diarrhea is the biggest cause of child mortality. The initiative has created specially designed packages, AidPods, which fit perfectly into the spaces between the bottles of Coke. It's a win–win.[2]

Why is this story a good example of the strategy of collaborating? Because the two parties together were able to achieve something that they could never have done alone. At the same time, it benefited them both. ColaLife was able to use this method to distribute medication, while the initiative was great news for Coca-Cola's image.

A builder had to repair some paving in a school playground. While the children were in class, he taped off the work area and got to work. But at recess, the children came running outside and interrupted him. Paying no heed to the tape, they stepped over and swarmed him. When he tried to shoo them away, they paid no attention. The recess lasted an hour and he couldn't afford to lose all that time. So he turned the children into assistants, asking them to hand him the tiles for laying. They set to work with enthusiasm and the job was finished in no time.[3]

The management team of a Dutch company wanted to reorganize its purchasing department but, in the Netherlands, such changes must be approved by a Central Works Council (CWC), which represents employees' interests, and the company's CWC flatly rejected the proposal. Generally such a conflict would be resolved through legal action. But the management team instead asked the CWC to explain exactly what was wrong with the plans. The CWC came up with a laundry list of issues. What was the management team's response? They agreed with the CWC completely. Not as a trick, but because they shared the same goal of making the department run better, and the CWC had important insights. The members of the CWC were—literally—speechless. They were so used to a mode of fight and conflict that they were blown away by something in essence very simple and noncombative: honest curiosity. One simple question had revealed that the management team and CWC were completely in agreement, and after that the necessary changes were carried out smoothly.[4]

Paying careful consideration to common interests can change even the most notorious enemy into an ally. For example, one girl I interviewed on my Flip Thinking podcast used to get quite upset about a classmate's gossiping. Many class members had thought that this classmate would keep a secret for them and had been quickly disavowed of that illusion; everything was shared right away. During the podcast we decided to turn the situation to her advantage. She had decided that she wanted to come out to the class as a lesbian, but she didn't want to have umpteen conversations with her classmates about it. So she shared the news only once—with the notorious gossip, as a "secret" of course, and in no time the whole class knew. The girl reported that her classmates "could hardly have been more positive."[5]

My company conducted a two-day flip-thinking event with the management and board of Reclassering Nederland (Probation of the Netherlands), a national foundation that works with people on probation, providing opportunities such as community service. We explained the various flip-thinking strategies to the attendees and we asked them to use their intuition to choose the strategy from which they could most benefit at that moment. A majority vote selected the strategy of collaborating. Why? Who was their enemy? The answer was simple: the press. The service had been in the news recently regarding a number of problem cases. The group decided to make the press its partner. "After all," the participants said, "every theater group, commercial business, and political party would be delighted with so much media attention. Let's use it to our advantage!" A few days later the chair of the board of directors of the organization, Sjef van Gennip, requested an interview with a national newspaper. What was the result? A front-page article, which introduced the organization's plan for improving its services, "with a few catches," Van Gennip conceded about some points of criticism in the piece. "But Reclassering did want to stir up some debate," he added. That was a goal of the paper too. The enemy became the ally!

For those in the entertainment industry, publicity is a lifeline. There's no such thing as bad publicity, as the saying goes, and the worst scenario is no publicity. Uri Geller, the "mentalist" who can bend spoons with his mind, came under fire from journalists for years. James Randi, Geller's most famous critic, has written no fewer than two books about him, which absolutely tore him to pieces. What was the effect of all these serious accusations? The complete opposite of their intention! The eternal discussion in the press about whether Uri Geller was fake or not contributed largely to his success. It was thanks to all the attention, buzz, and rumors that his name reached a magical status.

To apply the strategy of collaborating, you must be prepared to rethink your assumptions about a situation. Is there really a problem, or could it be your way of looking at the situation?

Another variant of the strategy of collaborating is to appeal to an adversary's better nature by asking them for help, advice, or even a favor. Most people are keen to show off their good side. When Steven Spielberg was about 13, he was constantly tormented by a burly boy from his neighborhood, who looked something like John Wayne. "He would knock me down on the grass, or hold my head in the drinking fountain, or push my face in the dirt and give me bloody noses when we had to play football in Phys. Ed.," Spielberg recalled. Realizing that he would never be able to win a fight with the boy, Spielberg decided to try another tack. He asked him for a favor. Already involved in making films, he said to the boy, "I'm trying to make a movie about fighting the Nazis, and I want you to play this war hero." At first the boy laughed in his face, but then he agreed to take on the role, and ultimately he did all sorts of other tasks as well during filming. In the end he became Spielberg's best friend.[6]

In the late 1970s, in the Dutch town of Bussum, a shopkeeper used a similar method to tackle theft from his shop. The old man who ran the grocery shop had a problem: a group of local brats regularly stole sweets from the shop. The customers thought that the grocer should simply forbid them to set foot in the shop again, but he came up with another plan. One day, the most hostile of the kids was again hanging around the shop "inconspicuously." The grocer said to him, "I've got to go out back for a minute. Could you keep an eye on the shop please, because I often have sweets stolen by some children who come in here?" The boy nodded and stationed himself like a bouncer in front of the counter. According to the grocer, the boy never again stole anything from his shop.[7]

Another way of collaborating with a perceived enemy is to give him an *honorable retreat,* to build a "golden bridge" for him, as it were. There's nothing worse than being humiliated and having to eat humble pie. If you can give someone an appealing option for retreating from a conflict, they'll often leap at the chance to resolve the problem and keep their head held high.

In Sebastian Bailey and Octavius Black's book *Mind Gym,* they cite a great example of this honorable retreat. An employee and a boss were locked in conflict. One of them had to go, but neither wanted to leave. Since the boss had the advantage, the employee decided to sign up with a recruitment agency. But he had second thoughts, and the next day he went back to the agency and sang his boss's praises. A few days later his boss was headhunted by the agency, and soon he was offered a better job at another company. The boss resigned right away. He'd gotten his golden bridge, and the employee could happily stay where he was.[8]

A particularly refined method of collaborating is the *problem exchange:* something that's a problem for one person might well be an opportunity for another. For example: young Brazilians are keen to learn English, but taking classes is expensive. Meanwhile, many elderly Americans are quite socially isolated and would love to have someone to whom to talk. The CNA Speaking Exchange Project connects the two groups, brilliantly exchanging their problems.

The 115-year-old Cathedral of Saint Bavo in the Dutch city of Haarlem had a heating problem, facing an annual heating bill of $86,000 dollars. Meanwhile, a local IT firm had the opposite problem. Its computer equipment gave off a great deal of heat and it had to pay exorbitantly for cooling. Thus arose the solution of Holy Warming. The IT company installed its computers in the cathedral's cellar, which provides natural cooling, while also pumping the heat generated into the upper stories of the church.* In exactly the same way, the crematorium in Redditch in the Midlands of England was able to exchange its problem with the swimming pool next door. The crematorium management proposed to the municipal council that it use the heat of the crematorium to warm the pool. Despite fierce protests from some groups, the proposal was adopted, and it's estimated that the municipality will save $18,000 in energy charges annually.[9]

One quite special form of collaborating is what I call the *Frazier–Ali Doctrine,* by which enemies can use their antagonistic relationship to their mutual advantage. Boxers Joe Frazier and Muhammad Ali battled it out several times during their lives, becoming arch rivals—and not only in the ring. Muham-

---

* In the US, Microsoft engineers are working with scientists from the University of Virginia to create a similar plan to use computers in data centers as data furnaces to heat homes.

mad Ali called Frazier a "gorilla" and "Uncle Tom," because he thought Frazier wasn't doing enough to support the Civil Rights Movement. Frazier wasn't as sharp-tongued as Ali, but when his opponent was diagnosed with Parkinson's disease years later, he took the opportunity to speak out. "God's judgment," he called it. A few years later, as Muhammad Ali's condition worsened, Frazier said, "I believe I won our last fight." What effect did their cruel altercations have? Of course they deeply hurt one another. But in the end their bitter rivalry also helped build their celebrity worldwide. By fighting one another and publicizing their rivalry both in and out of the ring, they were helping one another on a different level to become legends. To get there, they more or less subconsciously collaborated with each other to build the public image of their rivalry.

During election campaigns in countries with multi-party systems, two parties being perceived as "the enemy" of each other can boost support for them both. The Netherlands has many political parties, and in 2010, the Labor Party, PvdA, and the conservative People's Party, VVD, both succeeded in drawing voters from the other parties. How? They fiercely attacked one another; the hostility worked to both parties' benefit because the fiercer the fights between them, the more attention focused on them, drawing it away from all the other parties. The political spectrum was reduced to a pure left–right contrast between these two parties. Then to the great surprise of many voters, following the election, the two warring parties entered into negotiations good-humoredly and very quickly formed a cabinet that promised to work in cooperation and the pursuit of "common interests."

A final form of collaborating is shamelessly *exploiting* the other. (Just to be clear, I'm not making any pronouncements on ethics in this book. Everyone is free to define their own limits; I simply show how mechanisms work.) This technique was used to flip-think the problem of being harassed by cold calls. We all get them, asking if we want to change our mobile phone plan, hawking a better cable offer, luring us to raise our credit card limit. Lee Beaumont from the city of Leeds in the north of England was so sick of them that he came up with a brilliant solution and now he wants to get as many of the calls as possible. He decided that he would only give his personal phone number to his family and friends, and for all companies, like banks and telecom providers, he set up a premium phone number. These numbers are for businesses providing a service, such as technology support, with callers charged for the calls and part of the fee going to the service provider. Each call makes Lee 13 cents a minute. He quickly earned more than $378 from calls, and he says he keeps the conversations going as long as he can to drive up the fees.

To round off this chapter, here's one last cheerful tale.

A 60-year-old woman in Belgium who suffered from Parkinson's disease fell over in her bathroom and couldn't get up. "I thought I was going to die that night," she told a Belgian newspaper, *De Standaard*. "I was stretched on the ground. My muscles, my back and my head were all hurting so much. I pulled a towel over myself to keep warm." After a few hours she was woken up by strange noises inside her house. Thinking it was the police, she shouted for help. It turned out to be two burglars. The woman repeatedly asked them to help her, and one finally did, calling the emergency services. The police came within ten minutes, so the burglars had to flee without getting their loot.

The strategy of enticing

What do you want a meaning for?
Life is a desire, not a meaning.
—Charlie Chaplin

Here's a story from back in the Dark Ages of computers. In the late eighties a British Airways department was set to make the move to computers. Most of the department's staff considered the transition a threat. What was this going to mean for their old, familiar working methods? Would they be given enough training? Several meetings to discuss the issue were held, but employees were still resisting. How could they be brought around?

Why do we take action? In essence, only for two reasons: because we desire something or because we're afraid of something. It's simple. Love versus fear. Desire versus aversion. Yes-and versus yes-but.

So which is the better motivator, fear or desire? We know almost instinctively that, in general, people are motivated more powerfully by fear than by reward. When we don't feel safe, when we're afraid of something, we tend to act immediately. Safety is a basic necessity of life, so we prioritize it. Experienced managers and consultants know this. It's the basis of the strategy of the stick: if you don't do as we say, it's going to hurt. An often-used metaphor in Dutch is the "*brandende olieplatform*," or "burning oil platform" in English: if you can make employees understand how dangerous a business situation is, they will stop clinging to the status quo and leap into action. They'll jump off the platform straight into the sea; anything rather than burn alive. Managers bombard employees with threats: "If we don't improve results, we'll go bankrupt"; "It looks like we might have to let half the staff go." Does it work? Well, in the short term, definitely. People usually step up to the challenge. The problem is that, if fear is the only motivator, then once the worst danger has passed, people tend to revert to the norm.

That precise pattern is often observed in corporate change processes. Everyone is full of good intentions for a while, and people seem to be on board, but before long they begin pushing back. To get people to embrace change, you must motivate them not so much by what they don't want as what they *do* want. So how do you do that? How can you *make* people choose to want something?! Isn't that a contradiction in terms? As the old saying goes: you can lead a horse to water, but you can't make it drink.

Consider how British Airways dealt with the pushback about the introduction of computers. The company could have just taken a bullying approach, maybe even threatening to sack people who kept complaining. Instead, a computer was set up in a corner of the office and the staff were invited to check it out. They were so amazed by all the things it could do and how easy it was to use that they started asking whether they couldn't get their computers faster.

Fear can get people to take action for a short time, but desire can get people to make long-term changes. If people crave something profoundly, if they desire it intensely, then of their own accord they will do what's necessary (and will keep on doing it) to get it. Thus the *strategy of enticing* relies on touching others' hearts, igniting their desires.*

Desire is one of the most beautiful forces in life. Desire is genuine and authentic. Desiring something is one of the purest sensations that a person can feel. Desire is spontaneous, uncontrollable, and heartfelt. As the philosopher Ernst Bloch said,

> I have come to the conclusion that desire is man's only honest quality. Humans can lie about everything. Something fake can creep into everything. Love can be a sham, courtesy is just a question of upbringing. Helping can come from selfish motives, but man cannot manipulate desire. Man is his desire.[1]

I'm sitting in a quiet house outside the city while writing this book. When I look out the window I see a big, rolling meadow surrounded by a fence. In the corner of that meadow, not too far from me, is a small horse. It's one of those miniature breeds, chocolate brown with a white mane and an unruly forelock of hair hanging over its eyes. Despite the size of the meadow, he's usually standing in the same muddy spot in the corner, for hours on end, barely moving. But every now and then, like a bolt of lightning from a clear sky, he takes off running. And when I say running, I mean *running*. He tears back and forth across the meadow like a creature possessed. He is wildly exuberant, delighting in his great speed. It's almost as though there's a little skip in his step now and again. When he's had enough,

---

* I summarized this in another of my books, on flip thinking in parenting and education, as such: for us as parents, the trick is to shift our attention from what we don't want (the annoying behavior) to what the child does want (his or her desire).

he goes back to his corner. Watching him run is so moving for me. Clearly he is so full of energy and lust for life that he loves running for the sake of running. That is desire in its purest form.

The logical next questions are then: first, what do people desire, and second, how can we use that desire as a lever for flip-thinking problematic situations?

Much theory and research has been devoted to studying human desires. Abraham Maslow's famous pyramid organized them into a hierarchy, with basic needs, like food, shelter, at the bottom, and at the top the desire for self-actualization and making a meaningful contribution to humanity. Educational theory emphasizes three fundamental needs: relatedness, autonomy, and competence. Professor of psychology Robert Cialdini crafted his six "principles of persuasion" around our desire for reciprocity, commitment and consistency, social proof, authority, being liked, and goods that are scarce.

I've taken a flip-thinking approach to figuring out how to best leverage desire when trying to turn problems into opportunities. Rather than beginning with a theory I collected all the flip-thinking stories I had gathered over the years that involved enticing people and categorized them. This allowed me to distinguish four levers for making use of the strategy of enticing: scarcity, reciprocity, consistency, and autonomy.

The principle at play with *scarcity* is that people tend to desire things more strongly when they're in short supply. Scarcity is worse than something not being available at all. Much worse. If something is simply not available, well, bad luck, so be it. You get that. But if something is scarce, then some people can obtain it but we might not be able to. That drives us nuts. In general, the scarcer the product, the stronger the operation of this mechanism. Robert Cialdini has this to say about it:

We want something if it's scarce and we have to fight for it. Long lines of people outside the store? Hurry! A lover in the game? Fight! Selling your house? Find a new buyer! There's something physical about this excitement. Think of animals' appetites.[2]

Marketers use various types of scarcity messages to lure buyers—time scarcity ("today only," "sign up for another seminar before leaving the auditorium and receive a $500 discount," or "we are taking calls only until 10 P.M. tonight"); scarcity in volume ("only a few copies left," "while stocks last," "when they're gone, they're gone," "this may be the last time that the Rolling Stones play near you"); and scarcity in accessibility ("for club members only," "exclusively for subscribers").

Marketers have also made clever use of the lever of *reciprocity*. The desire for reciprocity is one of the strongest psychological mechanisms. We feel strongly that you get what you give. You scratch my back and I'll scratch yours. The power of this belief cannot be overestimated. Across all cultures, people who violate the principle of reciprocity are reviled, condemned as selfish and greedy. I still remember my father, eyes blazing, talking about a "friend" he had known for decades, who was a smoker but never had a pack of cigarettes on him and was always mooching. The anger with which my father would talk about this taught me an important rule as a child: if you take, you'd better give. Even groups of friends who profess not to care about exactly how much everyone on a night out together has paid, and who are rolling in money, tend to keep terrifyingly precise track of whether everyone has paid their share. While in relationships, the balance of give and take can be unequal, even for a long time, even if we much prefer it not be. Research even shows that if the balance between giving and taking in a relationship is skewed, both partners feel more lonely.[3] The psychologists Pieternel Dijkstra and Gert Jan Mulder write, "The idea that giving and taking should ideally be in balance goes against the idea that some people have that friendship (or more generally, love) should be unconditional. That is indeed a very romantic and noble idea, but it doesn't reflect reality."[4]

The mechanism of reciprocity explains why scientists get free trips, why free samples in supermarkets work, and why businesses spend so much money on gifts to vendors and corporate outings. Those who receive these perks feel obliged to give something back for them, whether that's a favorable critique of a new drug, the purchase of some of that lovely cheese sampled, or extra hours worked. The mechanism also explains why we often find it difficult to accept something "just because." We intuitively feel that there's no such thing as "just because" and that, one way or another, something will be expected in return.

This strategy can also be used in reverse. Some new residents to a neighborhood were troubled that a man who lived on their street was regularly hassled by the local teenagers. They devised an ingenious solution; they decided to reward the teens for their bullying. They approached the teenagers and said, "We need your help. We really don't like that guy at all. We can pay you 11 dollars a day each if you want to make his life really unpleasant." The bullies were all ears, and the deal was struck. Their badgering increased enormously. After a few weeks, the "sponsors" went back to the bullies and said they were a bit short on cash and would have to stop the payments, but asked if the teens would please keep up their bullying of the guy anyway. The bullies were indignant. Are you kidding?! You think we're going to work for no pay! The bullying stopped.[5]

The mechanism of reciprocity is so powerful that it's even able to save lives. The scientist Irenäus Eibl-Eibesfeldt tells the story of a German soldier in the First World War who was an expert at capturing enemy soldiers on their own side of the line. One day the German once again succeeded in surprising an enemy soldier. The unsuspecting man was sitting eating a piece of bread. What did he do when taken by surprise? In total panic, he offered the German a piece of his bread. The German was so confused by this bizarre offer that he let the other soldier be, turned around, and returned to his own lines.[6]

The third lever for enticing is the desire for *consistency*. People want to be viewed as being consistent, and they also expect it of others. We want people to do what they say they'll do, and also not change their story every five minutes. People we perceive as being inconsistent are considered "unreliable," even irrational. By contrast, consistent people are seen as steadfast and eminently rational. No wonder; a society in which people behave according to commitments functions considerably more smoothly than one in which commitments are treated as mere intentions. The value principle of consistency is so deeply rooted in human culture that it's an extremely powerful means of influencing people.

Once again, marketers are masters of the craft. One technique they employ is asking a series of questions to which the answer is sure to be "yes," called "getting someone into a yes-rhythm." Once you've said "yes" a few times, it's harder to say "no" to a subsequent question. That's true even when the "yeses" have got nothing to do with each other. Let's say a refrigerator salesman wants to sell a fridge that's larger, and pricier, than that which a customer is looking for. He might open with the question, "Sir, do you enjoy a beer now and then?" There's a good chance the customer will answer, "Uh, yes I do." The salesman follows up immediately with, "And do you like your beer to be nice and cold?" Again, the customer answers, "Yes." Nobody likes a warm beer. The salesman next asks, "Do you ever drink beer with friends, at home?" The customer doesn't need to answer anymore, a nod is sufficient. "And so do you like it when you've got plenty of nice cold beer sitting in the fridge, all ready to go, without your wife complaining that there's no room left over for anything else?" Naturally the customer agrees and the salesman pounces, "So, shall I put you down for this amazing deal while it still lasts?" (Why not throw in some scarcity too?)

Complimenting people is a clever variant of the consistency technique. If a boss compliments an employee on his efficiency, the employee will want to be seen consistently that way and will try hard to be very efficient. A very effective form of complimenting is to flatter an adversary. One way to do this is by asking them for a favor. It seems paradoxical, but the logic is exquisite. By asking for them to help you, you send a message that you consider them to be a big enough person to look past your differences. They will want to behave consistently with that assessment. When Benjamin Franklin was a member of the Pennsylvania legislature, he had continual conflicts with a particular political opponent. However respectfully Franklin behaved to the man, he was always extremely hostile in return. Every attempt at reconciliation was met with cynicism. Then Franklin tried a new approach. He knew that the man had a very rare book in his personal library. Franklin sent him a written request to borrow the book, and the man immediately had the book delivered to Franklin. In turn, Franklin returned the book a week later, accompanied by an elaborate letter of thanks. And what happened next? Relations between the two thawed, and eventually they developed a friendship that was to last longer than their political careers.[7]

However rational we think we are, our desires are unfortunately fed by a host of irrational considerations. What do we desire the most? We desire what is forbidden. Why? Because being forbidden violates our sense of *autonomy,* self-determination, the idea that we make our own decisions. This is why it's often ineffective—or more than that, counterproductive—to forbid teenagers to drink alcohol or use drugs. The ban fosters desire. The stricter the prohibition, the more desirable whatever's forbidden becomes. This means that prohibiting things, or denying people access to them, can be an effective strategy for making people want them even more.

The fourth technique, leveraging the desire for autonomy, doesn't have to involve any prohibition, though. When our children were younger, vacations were always a disaster. One wanted to do one thing, the others wanted to do their own thing, or something else entirely. It was a huge hassle to find activities everyone would enjoy. The result was lots of grumbling, and lots of irritation for mom and dad. Finally, we came up with the idea of all making wish lists and doing our best to let everyone fulfill their greatest desire for that vacation. To our surprise, lots of the things listed weren't the types of activities we'd expected, like going to an amusement park, but were simple things like having a certain food for dinner. We used these wish lists to create one special day for each person, in which everything was all about them. To our gratification, this had two positive effects: everyone had his or her own special day and, as an unexpected side effect, we discovered we all really enjoyed treating the others to a special day.

An acquaintance suggested a great use of the autonomy technique to my partner and me, for getting our kids to eat vegetables. Like most children, ours didn't like vegetables, but they did love pancakes. So he suggested we put some vegetables in the pancakes. We started putting spinach into the batter, and the boys ate the green pancakes without complaint. But this tip wouldn't be included in this book if the story had ended there. After all, the strategy of sneaking vegetables into favorite foods is now well-known. The real flip-thinking moment came only a few years later. One day we served ordinary pancakes, and the boys were having none of them. Yuck, who would want those weird pale-yellow pancakes? Weren't there any normal ones?

Our desires can be used against us as well as for good. This is unfortunate, but it's a fact. So we should flip-think this by accepting that fact and focusing on the opportunities in leveraging people's desires. Of course, the difficult thing is that what people desire isn't always obvious. Sometimes they don't even really know themselves, or they don't want to say. Revealing your desires makes you vulnerable. The good news is that if we work at it, we can often discover even people's wildest hidden desires. To illustrate, I'll close with the story of Griffin Hospital in Derby, Connecticut. The beauty of this story is that the technique used was extremely simple, while the results were unprecedented.

Things weren't going well for the hospital, and the board of governors had tasked a new CEO, Patrick Charmel, with building a new maternity wing so Griffin could compete better with other hospitals. Charmel started by conducting a survey of women who had given birth in the hospital, asking what would their ideal delivery room look like. The women expressed all sorts of unexpected desires, from being able to have partners stay overnight, to grandparents being allowed into the room during the birth, special play areas for children, Jacuzzis, and kitchens where families could prepare their own meals. The list of desires was so exotic that no hospital even came close to meeting them all. So what did Charmel do? He set himself the goal of fulfilling all of the wishes. Double beds for hospitals to accommodate partners weren't available, so Charmel had them made. Jacuzzis were said to cause infections, but he investigated and this turned out to be a myth. In the end, Charmel was able to fulfill almost all the desires. Patients raved about the new wing. The ward had a more positive, caring atmosphere. Was there some chaos and hassle? Of course, such as when families organized parties. Some of the staff even resigned. But they were replaced by better ones! The new facility proved to be a big draw for new, patient-friendly staff. The project was a huge success not only in terms of patient satisfaction, which rose to 96 percent, an unprecedented score in the healthcare sector, but also in terms of profits. The hospital climbed out of the red and before long had enough surplus to redesign the rest of the hospital along the same lines. Over the years, Griffin received dozens of awards, including a mention in *Fortune* magazine: 100 Best Companies to Work For. In 2008, the hospital was mentioned in this Top 100 for the ninth consecutive year, something that no other hospital in the United States has ever achieved.[8]

Play

Strategies 12 to 15

The strategy of flaunting

The strategy of role reversal

The strategy of disrupting

The strategy of reversing

Strategies that have "play" as their starting point
are based on the insight that the person who makes the
rules is usually the one who wins the game. Sometimes
the fastest way to flip-think a problem is by changing
the rules of the game. These strategies emphasize
creativity, intelligence, and humor.

The strategy of flaunting

All people play a role, except perhaps for a few actors.

Fairly often in Kentucky the limestone under the ground is washed away by water and a huge sinkhole is created, sometimes gobbling up whole houses. On February 12, 2014, it happened to the state's Corvette Museum. Video footage shows a hole measuring 39 x 32 feet developing within a few minutes and no fewer than eight Corvettes disappearing into the hole. It looked like the disaster would spell the end for the museum, and the management rushed to find ways to raise money to fill in the sinkhole. But then they reconsidered, because the sinkhole with the Corvettes sticking out of it quickly became a major tourist draw. Since the disaster, visits have risen by 60 percent, without additional advertising. The museum even sells T-shirts and post-cards displaying a photograph of the sinkhole.

I was originally a theater director, and I learned that one of the great things about working in theater is that it teaches you to accept problems. Let's say that an actor walks on stage for an improvisation and says, "Grrr, grrr, I'm a bear." It obviously wouldn't work if the fellow actor responded with "Actually you look more like a rabbit." Or, "You're so not a bear, you're an actor." Refusing to accept whatever transpires on stage spells the death of a scene.

But not only do actors learn to accept problems, playwrights and screenwriters make great use of them. In fact, they love problems. They're the fuel for compelling drama. Audiences love to sit in comfort, ideally with a beer or glass of wine in hand, watching a hero stress out. A good rule for coming up with an exciting script is to think of something that you personally would never want to experience, under any circumstances, and have your protagonist spend 90 minutes waging a passionate battle against it.

Problems in real life have consequences. That's not true with acting. It's a safe environment for having problems. At 9:25 P.M. an actor may be raging to the heavens over the death of his lover, and at 9:32 P.M. be in the green room, beer in hand, chatting about a great party he went to. A side benefit of the profession is that you learn to play along with problems. It gives you the feeling that you can ride problems out, like you can ride a skittish horse. You learn to look at problems from all angles. Playing with them gives you control over them and you discover that you're not defined by your problems, you *have* them and you can do all sorts of things with them.

This brings us to the twelfth strategy, that of *flaunting*. With this strategy you show off what you would usually want to hide.

Once, I was late for a training session. Fortunately, I knew the group had a good sense of humor. When I got there I said to them, "Obviously I'm very sorry that I'm 15 minutes late. I could try to skip some of the session, but instead why don't we do this? Set your watches back 15 minutes, then take your bags and your coats and leave the room, and I'll get prepared. [I use a number of props.] Come back in when I say so. I promise you that I'll present a session that's 15 minutes shorter, but with 15 minutes more content. Is that OK?" The group was happy to agree and played along enthusiastically. One of the participants even apologized for returning late.

Normally, when we have a problem we're inclined to hide it, which can result in extremely awkward situations. Stutterers know this better than anyone. The harder they try to stop stuttering, the worse the problem gets. As a great saying goes: stuttering is everything you do trying not to stutter. It's a perfect example of a vicious circle, a self-reinforcing system. Psychologist Paul Watzlawick describes successfully treating a stuttering salesman. He had the man deliberately try to stutter, to imitate himself as accurately as he could. The more the salesman tried to imitate the stuttering, the more fluently he spoke.

The essence of the strategy of flaunting is simple: display the problem, rather than hiding it. The great thing is that we can apply this strategy to many different areas of our lives. In fact, our tendency to hide problems is so strong that the opposite reflex, deliberately flaunting them, is perhaps one of the most effective flip-thinking strategies of all. If you employ this strategy, you will notice that life becomes much more fun, light-hearted, and creative—both for you and for the people around you.

My identification of this strategy was also based on analysis of a host of examples, and it was hard to choose those to offer here. When it comes to flaunting, one story is even more surprising than the next. So for this portion of the book I've focused on a small collection of stories, which represent four key approaches. The first is illustrated by the story of the Corvette Museum: treating the disaster as the intention. Don't try to fix the problem, work with it. Another example is that of a textile printing business on the Hawaiian island of Kauai. When Hurricane Iniki struck in 1992, the business suffered serious damage from the water and red dirt the storm brought with it. All the white T-shirts for printing were wet and filthy. Rather than throwing them away, the company decided to dry them out, red mud stains and all. This produced a unique cognac-colored background that they printed with typically Hawaiian texts and images. These "Red Dirt Shirts" were such a success that the business began to specialize in dyeing textiles with mud.

Perhaps an even more drastic example of the *disaster-is-the-intention approach* took place in New Zealand. During an earthquake, Phil Johnson's Christchurch garage was hit by a giant boulder, weighing some 25 tons. The stone fell through the roof and blocked the exit. It was a disaster. Not only was there a huge amount of damage, but Phil was saddled with a stone that wasn't going to be easy to get rid of. So what did he do? He affectionately dubbed the stone "Rocky" and . . . put it up for sale on Trade Me. Alongside a photo of the rock, Phil included convincing promotional text in which he explained—very humorously—why the rock was a fantastic investment. His ad quickly racked up hundreds of comments, including many stone-related jokes. Phil's unusual auction eventually made worldwide news. And how did the story end? On March 4, 2011, the auction closed with a bid of no less than NZ $60,050 (around US $42,000).* What's more, the winning bidder had to take care of collecting the stone, a condition Phil had put in the small print of his ad.

A second variant of the strategy of flaunting is one I describe as the *if-you-can't-hide-it-paint-it-red strategy*. Elton John has an eye condition, which requires him to wear glasses even when performing. Not exactly sexy. At first this looked like a negative for his career, but he turned it into a positive by making flamboyant glasses a trademark of his image.

Pouring a glass of Guinness is a time-consuming task. First, the bartender fills the glass three-quarters of the way, then waits,

---

* Phil Johnson stated that the money raised by selling Rocky would be donated to the local relief fund set up to help earthquake victims.

waits, waits until the foam head settles, and finally fills it up to the rim. That became a problem starting in the early 1990s as the pace of life picked up in so many ways. Pubgoers didn't want to wait for minutes on end for their beer to be ready, and sales of Guinness plummeted across Great Britain. The company ran commercials explaining the only "right" way to pour a Guinness, accompanied by slogans like "Good things come to those who wait" and "It takes 119.53 seconds to pour the perfect pint." "Not just anyone can pour a good pint," Guinness Master Brewer Fergal Murray said. Pulling a glass of Guinness became part of a holy pub ritual. Guinness won back its lost market share by flaunting the very thing that had, not long before, been the cause of its problems.[1]

One last example of this *paint-it-red* technique. Imagine that you run a budget hotel. How do you compete with other hotels? What did the Hans Brinker budget hotel in Amsterdam do? At the initiative of advertising agency KesselsKramer, the chain decided to lavishly emphasize the fact that they were a (very) budget brand by launching a campaign with the slogan "Come and sleep in the worst hotel in the world!" So what are the hotel's unique selling points? No parking, no sauna, no air-conditioning, no minibar, and no room service. The ads feature unashamed photos of rickety beds, dirty mattresses, and filthy showers. Backaches in the morning and the inedible breakfasts were featured, along with photos of how guests look before (bright-eyed and bushy-tailed) and after their stay in the hotel (hair all over the place and broken out in a rash). In one ad some of the letters in the neon sign on the front of the hotel aren't working, with the ad explaining, "We're focused on sustainability." The campaign is unstoppable. It's served for over 15 years now as a refreshing, often hilarious, draw for the chain.

I'd like to call the third approach to flaunting the *inferiority strategy*, after the English comedian, writer, and TV producer Stephen Merchant, who says, "I set myself up as inferior to the audience."[2] What he means by that is that, as a speaker, comedian, or actor, you should always adopt a lower status than your audience. Naturally you can make a clever remark, but it should always be from the position of underdog. How come? Because it makes you human. People are faster to feel sympathy for bunglers (in whom they recognize something of themselves; is there anyone who doesn't mess up now and then?) than for apparently successful types.

Talk show host David Letterman had a big problem. He'd had several secret affairs with female colleagues, and one day he received a letter in which the writer threatened to disclose these secret relationships unless Letterman paid him $2 million. Letterman responded to the blackmailer, a producer at CBS, by sending him a fake check. The man tried to deposit it and was arrested, and the case could have been settled. But Letterman decided to reveal the blackmail attempt and his sexual relationships on his show. "I feel like I need to protect these people. I need to certainly protect my family," he explained. He admitted his transgressions and offered his apologies to his wife, his colleagues, and the studio audience. The audience didn't boo him. They rewarded his candor with applause. What's more, the confession was an enormous hit. The episode became one of the show's most-watched episodes.

I call the final variant of the strategy of flaunting the *Sagrada Família approach,* named after the basilica in Barcelona designed by renowned architect Antoni Gaudí. Construction started in 1882, and moved at a glacial pace. Gaudí became so obsessed with working on the church that he didn't take any other assignments all the way until his death in 1926, and he actually lived on the site. Gaudí's artistic ambitions were so huge that construction was still unfinished on his death, and other architects took over the project when he died, continuing the work at the same slow pace and level of perfectionism. Construction is still underway. According to the current schedule, the church is unlikely to be completed by the hundredth anniversary of Gaudí's death, June 10, 2026. But has the church not being finished been a problem? Far from it; the basilica attracts millions of visitors each year, and the fact that it isn't finished is part of its legend. You could even say that the Sagrada Família stands to lose part of its magical appeal if it's ever completed.

What can we learn from the story of the Sagrada Família? It teaches us that it can be useful to shift our focus from the end product to the process itself, and that difficulties encountered along the way can be flaunted. As we've seen with great drama, we are sympathetic to those who struggle, who stumble and fall, but carry on. We may think that other people are chiefly interested in our successes, but they're at least as interested in our journey, particularly when it's been difficult, full of obstacles and requiring self-sacrifice. We can be almost certain that we will earn more sympathy, and admiration, by revealing these hardships than by hiding them. Think of how irritating it is when people go on and on about how successful their children are. We prefer to talk to people about the complexity of bringing up children. Successes can only be admired; worries can be shared.

Johnson & Johnson had struck gold with their painkiller Tylenol: it had a 37 percent market share and annual sales of $1.2 billion. But in 1982 the company faced disaster: Tylenol bottles in a number of Chicago retailers were contaminated with cyanide. Seven people died within a short period of time, and the perpetrator couldn't be found. All media outlets covered the incident and Tylenol's market share dropped immediately to just

7 percent. Analysts predicted that this would mean the end of the product, and perhaps even of the company. Yet despite all this, Johnson & Johnson was able to bring Tylenol's market share back to its previous level within six months, and the business's image was better than ever before. What was their secret? The leadership was aware that simply proclaiming the company's innocence and rejecting any responsibility would be the wrong strategy. The company instead opted for maximum transparency in addition to expressing a level of responsibility. Although the incident only affected Chicago, the product was recalled across the country: 31 million bottles were pulled from shops. CEO James Burke made himself available to the media, holding press conferences and appearing on news shows. He constantly emphasized that the company felt responsible for the incident, and a free call-in helpline was provided for customers to ask questions. Tylenol was reintroduced ten weeks after the incident, featuring new triple-sealed packaging.

The strategy proved a great success. Even President Ronald Reagan praised the company for demonstrating responsibility. Management courses consider Johnson & Johnson's response to the crisis to be *the* example of perfect crisis management.

We should never assume that our failures are unsurmountable problems. Always consider flaunting them. Here's one last example of how opportunity can rear its head even in an apparent disaster.

A nineteenth-century fresco of Jesus titled *Ecco Homo* (Behold the Man), in a church in the Spanish town of Borja, was extremely faded. An 81-year-old parishioner, Cecilia Giménez, took it upon herself to try to touch up the painting. She discovered that restoration is an art of its own. Her efforts proved disastrous, disfiguring the portrait so badly that some said the figure of Christ now looked like a monkey. The painting was dubbed *Ecco Mono*—Behold the Monkey. Critics declare the job the "worst restoration of all time." But was it really a disaster? Yes and no.

The municipality planned to hire a professional restorer to undo the damage, but an internet petition to keep the fresco as it was circulated, accumulating more than 18,000 signatures. The following summer, thousands of tourists flooded into the town to see the fresco for themselves. The church subsequently decided to ask tourists to pay to view the work, thus earning thousands of euros. Airline Ryanair even offered Spaniards discounted domestic flights to the town. An expert restoration could never have generated such a windfall for Borja.

The strategy of role reversal

*The only way to get them to come
to you is to let them go.*[1]

Imagine this. A man was about to go to bed when he spotted someone breaking into his shed. He rang the police right away, but was told that no officer was available. "As soon as someone is available, we'll send them." The man hung up, then called back again a minute later. "Hello," he said, "I just called you because there were thieves in my shed. But there's no rush now, because I've shot them." Within minutes half a dozen police cars were on the scene, along with helicopters and a firearms unit. The burglars were caught red-handed. "I thought you said that you'd shot them?!" one of the officers said to the man. "I thought you said nobody was available?!" he replied.

This story is a great example of the *strategy of role reversal*. In this strategy you break the existing role pattern by taking on the other person's role. In doing so, you force the other person to do the same: they then take over your role, and can begin to see things differently. I once performed a lecture for a school in the south of the Netherlands. A female teacher told me that, a few weeks earlier, one of her students had approached her indignantly. Why did he, a man, only score a six, while all the girls received a seven or higher? The teacher was about to argue with the boy, but instead decided to beat him at his own game. In an equally indignant tone she replied, "Yes, I was surprised too— real men usually get at least an eight." It was the boy's turn to be taken aback.

Pulling off a reversal requires some acting skill. You can't just do it—you have to do it convincingly. The other person has to truly believe you. In the case of the man whose shed was being burgled, he changed his tone from panicked to extremely off-hand. After all, he'd supposedly eliminated the danger. The police then flew into a panic, another role reversal!

Fortunately, acting is an ability many ordinary mortals possess. A friend of mine came across a small boy and his parents in a toy shop. The child was whining like crazy that he absolutely had to have a digital drum set. His parents didn't want to buy it for him, and they patiently explained that he'd just had his birthday and received lots of new toys, and that the drum set was expensive, and so on. He kept whining. When the parents said they wouldn't discuss it any more, the boy only whined even louder. By now the man witnessing this performance was strongly inclined to tell off the boy. "Hey! Didn't you hear your parents? No means no?!" Instead, he decided to declare his solidarity with the child. In a loud voice he said to the boy, "I couldn't help overhearing—wow, are your parents being ridiculous! It's just madness that they won't let you have that drum kit. You've really got a mean mother and father." Then he turned to the parents. "You two ought to be ashamed! Unbelievable." They all fell silent. The boy shrank into himself, moved a little closer to his mother and father and answered, almost inaudibly, "My mummy and daddy are really nice."

The strategy of role reversal doesn't need to involve such apparent impertinence. It also lends itself to very loving interventions. Take the case of a father helping his autistic daughter to brush her teeth. During a coaching session he explained to me the problem he was having with his daughter. The usual procedure was for him to check how well she had brushed her teeth and then finish the job properly for her. This was often difficult; after all, who wants someone peering into their mouth so intrusively? So, brushing her teeth became something of a daily battle. During the session we came up with the idea to change roles. What if he as her father would do the first brushing, and then his daughter would check how well he had done the job? In that case, his daughter would take the role of the expert. This is what they did after the coaching session and it worked out quite well. His daughter finally felt seen as a responsible individual, rather than a child being supervised. The result was exactly the same, but the process went much more smoothly.

Role reversal is simple in theory, but it can be tricky in practice. The reason it's so hard is that we are always inclined to do the opposite: not to go along with people, but to go against them. This pattern, in which we work against the other person's behavior, I call *contrasting*. Our behavior is the contrast to, the opposite of, the other person's behavior.

Here's an example. If someone wanders into the kitchen early in the morning looking rather tired and not quite fully awake, we have a tendency to react by being excessively perky. We'll say, "Good morning!" with exaggerated exuberance, or throw in a little sarcasm with "Good afternoon!" or "Oh look, it's Sleeping Beauty!" Maybe we'll even start trying to up the energy by doing funny walks around the kitchen (especially if we're a fan of the famous Monty Python "Ministry of Silly Walks" skit). What effect does this ribbing have? Usually it only makes the other person grumpy. Contrasting is another form of stuck thinking: once again, our attempt to solve a (supposed) problem backfires.

When people are demoralized we are inclined to cheer them up. When people are sad, we're inclined to get them into a good mood. When they're angry, we try to calm them down. When children are sitting quietly on the couch watching TV, we shout, "Get away from there and do something!" and when they're running around, we yell at them to "Calm down!"

The tragedy of contrasting is that it's always done with the best of intentions. That explains the phenomenon's persistence. We tell ourselves that we do it to help the other person but, if we're honest, we mainly do it to get rid of our own feelings of discomfort.

We tend to fall into the trap of seeing ourselves in contrasting roles in many situations, for example as helper versus the helped, or the victim versus the perpetrator, which usually makes problems worse. An aging mother may see herself as the victim of her son's neglect and fall into playing the role of victim, hoping that she will prod her son into playing the role of rescuer and coming to see her more often. But if she's complaining to him, she may push him further away.

The good news is that as soon as we recognize we're stuck in such a counterproductive pattern, we can use the strategy of role reversal to break out of it. A fan of flip thinking wrote to us about her experience of trying this with her 13-year-old son. He told her he needed her help studying for his math test, which he was worried about. His mother gladly played the role of tutor, but the tragedy was that the more the mother helped the boy with his problems, the more nervous he felt about the test. It was as if every explanation the mother offered confronted the boy with his own ignorance. On top of that, the mother was actually not at all good at math herself. She decided there was no need for contrast—she didn't have to be the authority. She thought, "What if I was to ask my son to switch roles: whether he could explain to me the mathematical formulas that he'd learned? After all, he knows more than I do . . . So that's what we did. A little later he was sitting next to me on the couch, very relaxed." He understood the material and could explain it to her quite well.[2]

Here's another case when contrasting only makes a problem worse. What happens when a somewhat messy man moves in with a fairly neat woman? They're likely to end up in greater contrast. The woman will probably clean up just that little bit sooner than she had done before, and the man will figure, well she'll clean it up before I get to it, so let her do it. So the woman ends up doing more and more of the cleaning. The vicious circle continues until eventually she's doing all the housework and telling her friends, "He doesn't do a thing."

An irony of contrasting is that it often means that the person who caused a problem, or has a problem, doesn't have to bear the burden of fixing things. Not only do we often take on their burden, but this is unhelpful to them. Acting as the helper, for example, can amplify the helplessness and dependency of the helped. Then they lose faith in their capacity to work out the problem on their own. Role reversal can break such negative patterns. It allows us to put the burden—in a very refined way—back where it belongs. By refusing to play an opposing role, you force the other person to take responsibility for the issue.

Let's say you're a doctor, and you give lectures to patients' associations on the responsible use of medicines. And let's say that your audience is extremely critical; they've had many bad experiences, and they distrust the medical professionals. How would you approach the situation? My first inclination would be to play the role of the responsible authority, who opposes their cynicism. But as we've seen, arguing with people often only makes them more set in their views.

A doctor, one of our followers online, who had faced this issue radically changed his approach. Rather than lecturing them, he started with a question. "What sorts of experiences have you had with doctors, pharmacists, and medicines?" They would regale him with stories of things gone wrong, but he wouldn't get defensive. He'd just say something like "Yes, that's really not good," or "Unfortunately that happens a lot." Eventually he said, "I can see that you all have a lot of experience already, a lot of it very bad. Today I'd like to tell you some things about how medicines work, and how you can ensure that you receive the maximum benefit from them. What could you do yourself to make sure that everything goes as well as it can?" He had put them in the position of authority over their medication. After that he started his lecture. The result? Everyone listened, and the mood was extremely positive and constructive. The mood remained positive even when the subject turned to less pleasant things like medicines that were no longer covered by insurance.[3]

The main aim of the strategy of role reversal is to break a counterproductive contrasting pattern. The most effective technique for this is *mirroring*. This is not always about showcasing negative behavior, it is also about genuinely putting yourself in the other person's shoes. The success of the doctor with his informative talks was due to him sympathetically mirroring his listeners' criticism of medical failures. When you mirror someone's concerns sincerely, you show people acceptance. You could look at mirroring as a form of empathy, or as "love-in-action."

One beauty of mirroring is that it can lead us to free ourselves from counterproductive roles. A woman once came over to me after a seminar and told me that her father was always complaining—about his health, about his home-care provider, and about the medicine he had to take. She played the role of listener to him, and she realized that maybe instead she should mirror his complaining. She asked if I thought she should start complaining to him about some of her own problems. "No, don't complain," I told her, "you need to really moan and groan! Get things off your chest. Put it all out there." She looked at me with some trepidation but said she would try it. A week later, she called me to tell me that the other day, before her father had gotten two sentences out, she had started to share her own complaints. "Oh, Dad, I can just imagine. It's like a madhouse here as well right now. The youngest has to go to the dentist, I've still got to help my oldest with his homework, my husband is late home and I've still got to put the dinner on . . ." After a few sentences she'd stopped for some breath, and her father had spoken the historic words, "That's terrible, love, is it always like that?" For more than 30 years she had played the role of supportive daughter for her father. Now for the first time she dared to break that pattern and her father was right there with her in under two minutes! "And," she went on, "perhaps the most important thing I learned is that I don't allow myself to complain. I always make myself put a brave face on it, be strong, play the good girl. I've realized that I don't want to do that anymore. I also want to be able to complain now and then."

Mirroring can instantly turn a tense situation around. I was asked to chair a debate for a hospital about their new mission statement. In a preparatory meeting with the head of communication and the head of public relations, they found it difficult to explain to me the purpose of the debate. Given that the executive board had commissioned the debate, we agreed that I would come back the following week to discuss their goals with them. I was given a lovely brochure on the new mission statement and a thick report about the work done to come up with it, and I went home.

A week later, I walked into the boardroom to find four men

seated behind the big oval table, and an empty chair in front, obviously intended for me. No one stood up to greet me or offered me coffee. I sat down. One of the men, who didn't introduce himself—I presumed he was the board chairman—said in a rather icy tone, "You wanted to talk to us?" That was it. Stone silence. How odd. It was as though they thought I was calling them to account, and they seemed quite hostile.

I decided to mirror his tone, saying somewhat petulantly, "Yes. I've no idea what the purpose of the debate is." Stone silence again. Then he responded brusquely, "You got the mission statement, didn't you?" I might have responded blandly along the lines of, "Yes, I've read it," but instead I ratcheted the brusque tone up still further, saying, "I asked you a normal question, surely you can just give me a normal answer?!" There was another short pause, and then my interrogator burst out laughing. I saw him wink at one of the other guys at the table, as if to say, "Well we've got a real character here, don't we!" The atmosphere thawed immediately, and we had a good discussion.

One of the great things about mirroring is that it allows you to get a feel for the other person's *needs*. What did the child studying for his math test need? To feel competent. What did the audience at the medical talk need? Their complaints to be taken seriously. What did the executive board of the hospital need? I discovered they were concerned that the mission statement wouldn't go over well with the staff. That uncertainty had caused them to be brusque toward me. They were being defensive because they anticipated I was going to be critical of the statement. By mirroring their tone, not only did I make clear to them how hostile they were being, but I picked up on their anxiety about what I might say.

At first glance the strategy of role reversal appears to be about coping with the other person's behavior, but it's also about ourselves. We and "the other" are far less separated than we tend to think. We're all connected to each other by invisible threads. Genuinely putting yourself in the other person's position, really trying to understand their perspective, can empower us to flip a situation by changing our own view of it as much as by changing their view. As Nelson Mandela put it, "Until I changed myself, I could not change others."

The strategy of disrupting

*The best way to solve a problem is
to discover the humor in it.*

Postal workers were up in arms. They had been told that they were no longer allowed to wear shorts during the warm summer months. It didn't take long to flip-think the problem: one of the workers came to work in a dress. Well, that was allowed, right?

Who determines the rules of the game? Paul Arden, author of numerous books about creative thinking, has this to say: "If you can't solve a problem, it's because you're playing by the rules." Which brings us to the penultimate strategy of this book: *disrupting*. It can be put to good use in situations in which the rules make a situation restrictive, oppressive, or stuck. This applies not only to explicit rules, such as laws and regulations, but to unwritten ones as well, which can be found in almost every situation. You could also call this strategy that of provoking, shocking, startling, obstructing, thwarting, or putting a wrench in the works. Just about anything goes, as long as it disrupts the other person's game. When that happens, a temporary vacuum is created, and new rules can be made. By us, obviously.

A great example of this strategy made world news in September 2004. The French government had just introduced a ban on "conspicuous religious symbols," targeted at the wearing of headscarves by Muslim women and girls. A 15-year-old Muslim girl from Strasbourg named Cennet Doganay wanted to respect, she said, "both the French law and the law of God." She had tried alternatives to a headscarf—a beret, a bandanna—but still the authorities refused to let her attend classes. So what did she do? She shaved her head, and was allowed into school, to much media hoopla. Imagine having such courage at just 15 years old.

Having a great sense of humor is hugely helpful with the strategy of disruption. People who take every situation seriously, who tend to color within the lines, have trouble with it. Jeffrey Wijnberg, who describes himself as a practitioner of "provocative psychology," is a great believer in playing with the rules of the game, particularly the unwritten rules between psychologist and patient. He finds there's nothing more effective than tripping the patient up in a refreshing, lighthearted way. For example, a man who came to see Wijnberg looked tired and was poorly groomed and badly dressed. He complained, "I don't know whether my wife still loves me." Wijnberg replied, "So you still have a wife then?" The man was confused. "Well," Wijnberg said, "when I see how disheveled you look coming into my office, I'm surprised that there's a woman who still wants to stay with you. Tell me, how do you manage that?" The man responded, "But I didn't come here to talk about why my wife is still with me." "Now listen to me, sir," Wijnberg replied with a great display of authority, "I'm the psychologist here, I know which question is best. So tell me, how do you do it?"

Provocative psychology is an interesting source of inspiration when it comes to the strategy of disrupting. This fresh and controversial psychology movement was created by the American Frank Farrelly. In 1974 he published the book *Provocative Therapy*, which outlined the principles of the movement. I've found two of those principles to be particularly useful for disrupting situations.

The first is called *red-green color blindness*. When a client would like to talk about something, in other words gives the green light to discuss it, the psychologist opts not to go into it. Conversely, if a client would prefer not to talk about something, giving the red light, the psychologist probes into it. Wijnberg deploys this technique with his disheveled client. When the man gives the red light to discussing the terrible state he's in, Wijnberg realizes that's all the more reason to press him about it.

The second technique is called *seesawing*. It is based on the fact that we all wrestle with inner contradictions, contradictory desires. We want the security of a guaranteed income, but we don't want to have to report to a boss. We want to start our own business, but we can't live with the uncertainty that comes with that. Most therapists choose to approach this sort of internal conflict from the position of a neutral observer, the objective analyst. The provocative psychologist, by contrast, without hesitation and with a great sense of drama, chooses one of the two opposing sides. "You're not sure about starting your own business? No wonder! I wouldn't do it if I were you. You wouldn't be able to handle the stress of the uncertainty. You're someone who needs security."* Almost inevitably, the client then pushes back. "But you know, I've been thinking about starting a business for so long, I really should go ahead and make the leap." How does the psychologist react? He seesaws cheerfully in the other direction. "That's true. Get things moving. Invest your savings. Even

---

* It's interesting to note that with this intervention, the psychologist applies the strategy of respect as well: he respects one of the two sides of the dilemma, but he doesn't express that position neutrally; he intensifies it. The therapist is in fact more in agreement with the client than the client himself could ever be.

though you've got a family to support, even though your wife has multiple sclerosis and can't work, surely your desires are important too? So what if you go bankrupt, you only live once! It's better to die on your feet than to live on your knees." If the psychologist perseveres this way, there's a good chance that the client will come back to a reconciliation of his own about the conflict he's in.[1]

The strategy of disrupting has enormous potential to transform difficult situations and stuck-thinking mindsets. After all, everything we do, think, design, have, decide, and experience is governed by rules. It's important to understand that these rules are not "the truth" or "simply the way things are." They're guides to living, much as a map is a guide to making one's way through a landscape but is not itself the landscape. Sometimes, though, the rules of the game seem so logical and natural that we think there's no other way things might operate. We think, "That's just how it's done." Is that a bad thing? Yes and no.

Let's deal with the "no" first. Acting in accordance with established rules is often extremely *efficient*. Want some light? Flip the switch! Greeting someone? You offer your hand. Eating? You do that with a knife and fork. Our lives are largely governed by these procedural if/then rules, and just imagine what life would be like without them. "Light? Um, wait, how does that work again? Flip the switch? Why, what does that do? Oh, it causes electrical current to flow to a lightbulb. But wait, why does the lightbulb generate light?" Parents may be familiar with such strings of questions from children who haven't yet learned all these daily rules. Imagine how awkward greeting someone could be. "Um, what do I do first? Take their coat? Say their name? Pat them on the head?" A great deal of our behavior is effectively automated—just think about driving a car. As I've said, that's extremely efficient.

A second reason why rules are useful is that they can actually be *life saving*. Lion? Run! Car coming? Don't cross the road! Something smells bad? Don't eat it! Some of these rules are innate, while others must be learned, because, while children often resist them at first—*why* do I have to go to sleep?—they are vital to living in our extremely complex societies.

Now the "yes"—the reason rules can be problematic. The answer is simple: some rules lead to stupid behavior. They are not well adapted to reality. Take the case of the *Sphex,* a type of wasp. When the female *Sphex* has laid her eggs, she goes in search of food in the form of caterpillars. As soon as she finds a caterpillar, she paralyzes it and drags it to the tunnel leading to her nest. The wasp then enters the tunnel without the caterpillar, to inspect the nest. If everything is in order, she returns to the caterpillar to drag it into the tunnel. No problem there. But if a researcher moves the caterpillar slightly out of the entrance to the tunnel while the wasp is in the nest, when the wasp comes back to retrieve the caterpillar, it instead repeats the ritual, putting the caterpillar back at the mouth of the tunnel and going to inspect the nest again. If you wanted to you could trap the wasp in an endless loop of mindless behavior by moving the caterpillar each time it enters the nest.[2]

Why do we follow rules so slavishly? Because they give us a sense of safety, a feeling of being in control, and of being approved of. This is perhaps why we tend to establish unspoken rules when explicit ones haven't been set forth, and why most of us adhere strictly to them. Though sometimes we have to learn them the hard way. This can sometimes give those of us who already know the rules a bit of *Schadenfreude*. Say at the office a box of assorted pastries is put in the coffee area for every staff birthday. There's always only one chocolate éclair in the box, and everyone knows it's reserved for Chris, the head of the department. Whenever a new colleague joins, the team gleefully anticipates what will happen when the next box of pastries is delivered. If the newcomer innocently picks up the chocolate éclair, someone will say, "That's for Chris!" The newcomer will drop the éclair in shame, and the next time will be gleefully anticipating the newcomer's faux pas.

Disrupting isn't just a matter of upsetting the rules; it's about eliminating them completely. And that's difficult. As we saw earlier, humans usually see more value in action (in doing something) than inaction—doctors prefer to operate rather than not to—and, similarly, we prefer to impose order on our lives rather than to risk that they might become disorderly. Yet our rules sometimes create more problems than resolutions. To give an example, our company works with trainers and actors who sometimes need to leave the house really early in order to get to work on time. We decided the company should cover the cost of an overnight stay if someone had to hit the road before 7 A.M. to make it on time. This was intended for instances when a job was considerably further away from the person's home than usual. But some people had to leave very early due to regular traffic jams near where they lived. Should an overnight stay be covered in that situation also? We changed the rule to "before 7 A.M., with exceptions," and we said we'd evaluate what would count as an exception on a case-by-case basis. We thought we'd worked it all out. But then two actors swapped a training session with each other. The one originally assigned to the session lived quite close to the location whereas the other lived farther and would have to leave before 7 A.M. They had exchanged on their own initiative, without consulting us, so did the company have to reimburse the cost of an overnight stay in this case? Or should the guy just accept that he would have to leave earlier? We debated the issue and realized that we could end up making all sorts of exceptions. Before we knew it, we'd be writing up an elaborate *Guide to Reimbursements for Trainers and Actors,* with a new appendix added each year. How absurd! That's bureaucracy, not efficiency. Which is exactly what you see with a lot of bigger companies: in their attempts to organize everything properly, they introduce lots of inefficiencies. It's a perfect example of stuck thinking.

At my company, we wondered how we could flip-think the situation. The answer was very simple: simply by *not* organizing it. We would decide what to do on a case-by-case basis. This may seem like a messy policy, but it's worked wonderfully and is in keeping with the kind of culture we want to nurture. We want to remain a fun, flexible, and creative company, not become the USSR.

It isn't just big businesses that love organizing things to the nth degree. Governments, too, are masters of this craft. Despite repeated initiatives to deregulate, the Dutch government continues to produce all sorts of rules and regulations. In June 2008 this caused a major outcry from Dutch public servants responsible for procuring goods and services. They had been confronted with a new 650-page-long public procurement act setting forth, in excruciating detail, the procedures to follow. Obviously the intentions were good; to prevent fraud and overpaying. But the consequence was outrage.

In one deregulation effort, the Dutch government started a campaign codenamed Purple Crocodile, after a popular advertisement in which a swimming-pool employee refused to return a purple crocodile toy to a mother and her child unless the mother filled out a form. What was the working group's first task? Believe it or not, drawing up the rules that deregulation had to follow! Even as I write that, it seems made up, the perfect punchline, but unfortunately it's true.

Robert Fritz, the creativity expert, makes an urgent appeal not to go looking for rules for the sake of rules. He has this to say about it:

> Some people hope to find the right system, the right method, the right approach and the right regime. They think that if they just apply these rules, things will work out well for them. For these people, the extent to which they follow the rules is a test of their sincerity. They cite "authorities," such as authors, experts and specialists, to vindicate the correctness of their approach. They get insecure when faced with people who can improvise, innovate and break all the "rules" on their way to success.[3]

So the crucial question is: how can we break free from misguided rules? Psychologist Edward de Bono suggested the "po" method. "Po" refers to a "provocation operation" of some kind, a bold, perhaps seemingly absurd idea that prompts creative problem solving. As an illustration, in the early 1970s the New York Police Department consulted de Bono on the city's growing crime rate. Familiar policies like tougher punishments and more police on the streets didn't seem to be working. De Bono put forward the provocation, the po: police have six eyes. The initial response was bewilderment. But after some consideration, the idea of using civilians as extra eyes for the police came up, and the neighborhood watch was born. Since that time, the practice has been implemented all around the world.[4]

A second way of challenging rules is to follow any statement of a rule with "Oh yeah?" "Cars have four wheels." "Oh yeah?" Who says? So cars can't have three wheels? Or five? Or none? Questioning one thing enables us to disrupt and flip-think everything.

Here's a rule: a prescription medicine should have a proven active ingredient. Oh yeah? A pharmacy in Watford City, North Dakota, made news prescribing Monster Spray to cure children of their fear of monsters. It comes in a bottle with an official-looking label instructing users to "Spray around the room at night before bed, repeat if necessary." Apparently it works wonders. How eminently logical. After all, if you should fight a real condition with a real medicine, why shouldn't you fight a condition only of the mind with an imaginary medicine?

Here's another rule: graffiti on buildings, buses, and trains are an eyesore and all of it should be removed. Oh yeah? What about *reverse graffiti*. What's that? It's created by placing a template of an illustration or text on a dirty surface and blasting the surface with a high-pressure water jet to clean the cut-out areas of the template, creating a design by the contrast. You're not spraying anything on, you're spraying dirt off, so, for this reason, reverse graffiti is also known as clean graffiti. The great thing is that this type of graffiti is of course extremely environmentally friendly. Companies like Microsoft, the BBC, Smirnoff, Kia, and Puma have carried out advertising campaigns using this technique, and it was used in Barack Obama's presidential campaign.

The strategy of disrupting can help even with extremely difficult situations. A nurse who worked in an emergency psychiatry department emailed me to explain how he used it to come up with a new way of subduing unruly patients. Some could be so aggressive that as many as six staff members would be required to restrain them, and then the patient would be put into an isolation room. That struck the nurse as inhumane. He convinced his colleagues to try something radically different. When a patient had been subdued, he would walk in, look the patient in the eyes, and ask in a very friendly way, "Would you like a sausage roll?" Often, patients hadn't eaten for some time. Most patients immediately responded by calming down. The organization has had great success with this method, and it helped to cut down on patients being confined in isolation.[5]

During the late 1970s and 1980s in America, the Black preacher Wade Watts, Oklahoma state president of the National Association for the Advancement of Colored People, was constantly antagonized by former wrestler and the leader of the Ku Klux Klan Oklahoma arm, Johnny Lee Clary. During one encounter, Clary and about 30 associates clad in white KKK robes and conical hats cornered Watts in a restaurant as he was eating a plate of fried chicken. "Whatever you do to that chicken," Clary said threateningly, "we're going to do to you!" A short silence followed. What could Watts do? Or better, what could he do to disrupt the situation to his advantage? I don't know what you would do—I would be terrified, I'm pretty sure—but I know what Watts did. He kissed the chicken! Laughter erupted around the room, including from some of the Klan members. Furious, Clary sent his men outside.

Fortunately even the business world, usually so buttoned up, is becoming increasingly aware of the possibilities presented by the strategy of disrupting. The chain of HEMA department stores in the Netherlands used it to raise awareness of the problem of shoplifting in their stores. The retailer hadn't been able to get the press to cover the problem. Then the chain came up with the idea of temporarily dropping the prices of the five most-stolen items by 25 percent. Special displays were stocked with the five products—bottles of dietary supplements were the most popular, followed by rechargeable batteries, lip gloss, CD-Rs, and bike lights. A sign above read TOP 5 MOST NICKED. The displays were heavily protected by additional security cameras. The stunt generated national publicity for the problem of shoplifting, just as HEMA wanted.[6]

Governments, too, are awakening to the wisdom of disruption, doing away with counterproductive rules. In the Dutch town of Drachten a major roundabout was the scene of frequent accidents. Some of them were very severe. All attempts to make the roundabout safer—extra traffic signs and lights—didn't work or, even worse, made the roundabout more chaotic and unclear. A typical example of stuck thinking. Hans Monderman, also known as the "Paganini of traffic engineering," after the great violin virtuoso, was asked to solve the problem. He proposed a radical idea: not to do more, but to do less: remove all the traffic signs and lights. The result? From then on people carefully approached the roundabout, drivers as well as cyclists and pedestrians. Instead of watching the signs and lights, they started watching one another. The number of accidents dropped dramatically and the traffic started to flow almost twice as quickly. By not trying to control it.[7] Monderman's philosophy has been adopted by many towns across Europe. The German town of Bohmte, for example, was granted 1.2 million euros by the European Union to conduct an experiment removing all traffic lights and signs from the town, which proved a huge success. Monderman's approach has been so successful that Drachten has become a place of pilgrimage for traffic engineers from around the world.

One last story.

Even when rules seem sensible, I mean *really* sensible, it may still be smarter to break them. The police once stopped me in the middle of the night. I had to show them my driver's license, and they called headquarters with my information and checked whether my car was stolen. They asked me whether I'd been smoking pot and looked in the trunk. I even had to take a breathalyzer test. The stop took about half an hour. When they told me I could go, I asked why they'd stopped me—were they looking for someone, had I done something suspicious, was I driving too fast? Their answer was a total surprise. I had kept too carefully to the speed limit. "The only people who keep to the speed limit on this road at this time of night," one of them said, "are either drunk, stoned, or criminals." Incredulous, I responded, "So I would have been better off driving faster than the speed limit?" Without missing a beat they answered in unison, "Yes."

The strategy of reversing

You've got to think lucky. If you fall into a mud hole,
check your back pocket—you might have caught a fish.
—Darrell Royal, American football player and coach

In Mark Twain's novel *The Adventures of Tom Sawyer,* when Tom gets into mischief yet again, his aunt Polly makes him white-wash a fence as punishment. It was a big job. "He surveyed the fence," Twain writes, "and all gladness left him and a deep melancholy settled down upon his spirit. Thirty yards of board fence nine feet high." But Tom is able to convince his friends that this chore is actually a sublime artistic pastime. They ply him with gifts so that they might be allowed to paint a section:

> Twelve marbles, part of a Jew's harp, a piece of blue bottle-glass to look through, a spool cannon, a key that wouldn't unlock anything, a fragment of chalk, a glass stopper of a decanter, a tin soldier, a couple of tadpoles, six firecrackers, a kitten with only one eye, a brass doorknob, a dog-collar—but no dog—the handle of a knife, four pieces of orange-peel, and a dilapidated old window sash.

Tom ends up lazing around the whole day long.[1]
Tom Sawyer is able to cunningly turn something undesirable

into something desirable. To do so he uses the final flip-thinking strategy, that of *reversing*. A problem is directly and immediately turned into an opportunity. It becomes the *intention*. A shortage becomes a windfall. A shortcoming becomes a talent. The strategy of reversing is perhaps the most wonderful strategy of all. It's when something that annoys or irritates you at one moment becomes a blessing in the next. All the energy of trying to solve the problem can now be harnessed to your benefit. This means that many disasters are potential blessings. Richard Wiseman, who in addition to being a psychologist and author is also a pretty good magician, describes how he lost his box of magic props one day. Panic! He had an important performance the next day. He was forced to use everyday items to come up with a new routine. The result? He invented one of his best tricks.

The strategy of reversing comes in many forms. I will call the first one *reframing*. You don't actually change the situation, you just change your view of it, like putting a more beautiful frame on a painting to make it look more valuable. Or a psychiatrist treating someone who suffers from insomnia by reframing. "Just think of how many people suffer from having a regular sleeping pattern," they might tell their patient. "They spend eight or nine hours each night doing nothing!"

One way of reframing is to change the language you use. The words we use reflect our thinking. In the chapter on the strategy of rethinking we saw that Richard Wiseman discovered that pessimists and optimists literally saw the world around them differently, with pessimists less likely than optimists to spot a £10 note left on the ground. Wiseman also discovered that optimists and pessimists describe the same situation differently. He presented groups of optimists and pessimists with the same scenario: "Imagine that you go to the bank and suddenly you find that you're in the middle of an armed robbery. Shots are fired and you get hit in the arm. How would you assess the situation?" What were the results? Almost without exception, the pessimists described the situation negatively, as "a disaster" or due to "bad luck," saying things like "That kind of thing always happens to me," while optimists considered that they'd benefited from "a blessing" in only being struck on the arm, saying things like "What a stroke of luck, I could have been killed!"[2]

Not only does the way we think influence our choice of words, but the words we choose inform the way we think. How do you ensure that information is passed on quickly? You can point out that the information is important, but people may not be impressed by that. In fact, if they believe that sharing the information is mostly in your own interest the effect can even be counterproductive. But what if you describe the information as "secret"? That immediately elevates it, and also entices people to pass it on.[3]

Political spin doctors know all too well the power of words to change perception. The term "mortgage interest relief" is a fairly neutral description of the policy that lets homeowners deduct mortgage interest from their income tax. What language did the Dutch Socialist Party use to discredit the policy? "Mansion subsidy." In the US, the movement against abortion calls itself not "anti-abortion" but "pro-life." Republican opponents of the tax on inherited wealth—neutrally described as "estate tax"— labeled it the "death tax."*

Words have power, so it's a good idea to carefully consider what the effect might be of any words you choose. For example, let's say that a manager "requests" that one of his staff take care of a particular task. This action could be described in a number

---

* The American linguist George Lakoff introduced the concept of framing in 2004 using these and other examples.

of other ways, maybe as a "command" or "demand." Family therapist Virginia Satir wisely suggests,

> Listen to what you say and see if you are really saying what you mean. Nine people out of ten can't remember what they said 60 seconds ago. [. . .] There are ten English words that it is well to pay close attention to, to use with caution and with loving care. I, you, they, it, but, yes, no, always, never, should, ought.[4]

Reframing doesn't always have to involve a change of wording though. Sometimes that isn't necessary. My partner and I hosted a foster son for two years. Every now and then he had a nightmare and would come into our bedroom sweaty and panicked. Not only were the nightmares themselves scary, he also became more and more afraid he would have one. Sometimes he lay awake for hours, scared to sleep. Eventually I said to him, "You've experienced bad things in the past, and now that you're a bit older and things are going better, you're having nightmares. For some people that only starts when they're about 20 or 30. So you're ahead of the game. That's actually a very good sign. And though nightmares are really scary, they can never be as scary as things were in real life. And you survived those things. So I say, bring the nightmares on, and let's get them over with!" The discussion did the trick. He only had one more nightmare after that, and we didn't know about it until he told us at breakfast. He hadn't felt the need to come into our room.

The essence of reframing is changing the way a situation is interpreted. This might include the way a word is interpreted. Some terms that were once slurs lose their negative connotations. The term Impressionism was originally derisive, given to the now beloved style of painting by a critic in a vicious review.

Cosmologist Fred Hoyle used the term "big bang" in 1950 as a sarcastic characterization of a theory of the origin of the universe put forward by Georges Lemaître that Hoyle found absurd. He was a proponent of the Steady State theory, which argues that the universe has always existed. That theory is now totally in disrepute and the Big Bang has become a household term, with the theory embraced by the scientific community and one of the best-known scientific concepts among the general public.

One final means of reframing to mention is the use of visual imagery. Advertising agency JWT Brazil collaborated with the A.C. Camargo Cancer Center in Brazil to devise a brilliant way to alleviate children's fears about chemotherapy. In cooperation with Warner Brothers, which owns DC Comics, the spooky-looking bags of chemicals used in the therapy were redesigned with plastic casings bearing the images of superheroes like Batman, Superman, Wonder Woman, and Green Lantern. The formula became a magic "super formula" as many superheroes have. The children were encouraged to see themselves as superheroes too. The entire children's ward was also decorated in a superhero theme.

The principle at the heart of a second variant of the strategy of reversing is captured in Dutch soccer player Johan Cruyff's oft-quoted statement "Every disadvantage has its advantage." The popular phrase a "blessing in disguise" expresses the same idea. Finding these blessings is a skill that seems to come more naturally to children. While adults tend to complain when it rains, children play in the puddles.

A number of years back, I was involved with the opening of a new housing complex in the Dutch city of Tiel. The organization in charge of the complex wanted to host a festive opening that would include a conference. The problem was that the closest location that was suitable for a conference was nearly two miles away from the complex. What could be done? Rent buses to shuttle people there? Provide bikes? Organize carpooling? Someone flip-thought the disadvantage into an advantage. Why not give the conference goers a guided tour of the city on the way? After the event the only negative comment was that the guided tour was so short!

While looking for the advantage in every disadvantage can be consciously applied to many situations, sometimes it's only after the fact that we realize we've reversed the problem and used it to our advantage. A Belgian student, living in the city of Antwerp, had trouble finding a place to live in Utrecht in the Netherlands. So she had to commute several hours a day. Fellow students felt sorry for her, and told her, "That wastes so much time," and "You won't be able to keep it up." So, she presumed she had a real, unsolvable problem. But how did she flip-think this? This is what she wrote to us: "The long commute forced me to make good use of the time by studying in the train. Due to the lack of distractions on the train, such as chatting with roommates, I completed all my assignments and rarely had to study once I got home. Consequently I kept up with the work at university better than I had ever managed to at secondary school."[5]

George Eastman, who founded the Kodak camera company in 1888, ran into a big problem with his first camera. It was a great device in many ways. It could take 100 photos with a roll of film and was very easy to use, with only two buttons: one to turn the camera on and off, and one to wind the film. But the design had a flaw. Eastman wanted to sell the camera to the mass public, and to keep the price as low as possible, he opted not to incorporate a mechanism that would have enabled users to change the film themselves. It was just too expensive. Eastman racked his brain to come up with a creative solution, which he did. It was based on not solving the problem and instead using it as an opportunity. He came up with a slogan that turned the camera's shortcoming into its strength. The motto? "You press the button, we do the rest." This flash of inspiration turned out to be extremely successful. In those days photography was still seen as a kind of magic. All sorts of things could go wrong during the process. Eastman's motto spoke to consumers' desire for assistance. And so Kodak very quickly became the biggest camera manufacturer in the world.[6]

At an individual level, too, being unable to solve a problem can sometimes be a huge gift. Getting fired; what's the good side of that? Burning out; what could you learn from that? Ending a relationship; what benefit might that have? Certainly sometimes a disaster is simply a disaster, but all of these difficulties often lead to new opportunities. It's not just systems that are antifragile, we are too. We have an enormous capacity to grow in response to setbacks. We possess an almost magical ability to reinvent ourselves. This requires giving your brain a push in the opposite direction—reverse it. Whenever you experience a misfortune, give yourself the mental assignment of redefining it as a blessing.

In 1962, the Doyle Dane Bernbach advertising agency was commissioned to come up with an advertising campaign for Avis. The car rental company was not doing well. Hertz was the clear market leader, and Avis, at number two, had just 11 percent of the market share. It looked like a David and Goliath situation. The agency realized that the typical advertising approach of championing how successful and popular the company was would be perceived as disingenuous; obvious false promotion. So the agency flip-thought, launching a campaign that used the fact that Avis was "only" number two as a selling point. They took out full-page ads like, "Avis is only No. 2 in rent a cars. So why go with us? We try harder. (When you're not the biggest, you have to.) We just can't afford dirty ashtrays. Or half-empty gas tanks. Or worn wipers. Or unwashed cars." They even turned the fact that they had fewer customers than Hertz into a positive. "Go with us next time. The line at our counter is shorter." The campaign was wildly successful. The company's market share grew more than threefold in four years. The key to success was the surprising honesty. Consumers expect ads to be deceptive in some way. But the claims made in the campaign about trying harder came across as credible. The ironic humor also helped.

The idea that *resisting* a problem almost by definition results in stuck thinking has been a main theme of this book. Flip thinking a negative quality, turning it into an opportunity, is the better approach. The question is, how? Simply taking the diametrically opposed view that people are fundamentally good certainly doesn't work. Speaking for myself, although I believe that, at the core, every human being is *inclined* toward good, in practice we're much more complicated. The "humans are good" view doesn't do justice to our contradictory nature. What's required for flip thinking a "shortcoming" into a "talent" is instead that we adopt a more neutral stance; neither that humans are "good" or "bad," but that "humans have capacities." These capacities aren't in themselves good or bad; they're qualities, skills. They help us to survive, both as individuals and as a species. *How* we use them is up to us. But the capacities in themselves aren't good or bad; they simply *are*.

Biologist and primatologist Frans de Waal emphasizes human complexity. He argues that human nature is characterized by a duality of aggressive and altruistic qualities, which has aided our species's survival. He raises the question where we would be *without* our aggressiveness. It has driven us to defend ourselves and our loved ones, to achieve success in business, and to make technological advances. We are highly evolved apes, and De Waal highlights that we've inherited both something of the good-natured, loving bonobo and the bullying, domineering chimpanzee, our two closest animal relations.[7]

Trying the reversing strategy forces your brain to go in search of "the good" in "the bad." Gavin de Becker, author of the influential book *The Gift of Fear,* has applied this to his own life perhaps like nobody else. He was subjected to horrible domestic violence as a child. Did he become an anxious, distrustful person? Yes and no. He certainly became distrustful and anxious. But over time, he turned that into a positive, helping us to learn how we can all harness our fear and sense of danger to protect ourselves. He is viewed as *the* violence-prevention expert in both the public and personal spheres, and runs a business that protects politicians, pop stars, and managers of *Fortune* 500 companies. He became a regular guest on *The Oprah Winfrey Show,* and he's written several bestselling books. What does he think of the human tendency to be scared or suspicious? He sees it as extremely positive and points out that we have an even better intuition for danger than dogs do. He argues that we mustn't suppress our fear but instead be highly attuned to it and use it to our advantage.[8]

Our society attaches great value to extroversion, perseverance, flexibility, and optimism. I won't try to claim that these qualities are not useful, even necessary; they are. But, on the reverse side, the opposite qualities are at least as useful; it's just that we're more inclined to see them as a handicap. What's so good about introversion, being quick to give up, inflexibility, or negativity? People who are more introverted are (much) more observant. If the governments involved in the futile trench warfare of the First World War had given up a bit earlier, millions of lives would have been saved. When it came to their principles, Mandela and Gandhi were extremely inflexible. Should they have been more flexible in that regard? Surely a healthy dose of negativity would have made the banking and credit crisis much less severe? What's wrong with keeping a worst-case scenario in mind?

We can apply this same flip thinking to a vast range of characteristics that are commonly seen as negative. Is your child not good at standing up for himself? Perhaps he's extremely empathic and is more interested in standing up for other people. Do you find it hard to make decisions quickly? What's wrong with being discerning? Impulsive decision making causes all sorts of problems. Do you tend to be gloomy? Is your child a sore loser? Perhaps he possesses a strong drive to succeed.* Obviously the art here is to examine our qualities honestly, both positives and negatives, not simply tell ourselves a fairy tale about who we are.

Fortunately as a society we are getting better and better at applying this way of thinking. In education, less emphasis is being placed on making up for shortcomings and more on reinforcing talents. Dyslexic children are no longer expected to just struggle through and learn to read and write along with everyone else; they're offered tutoring. We are at the dawn of a new era in making this flip. We know that some autistic people can pay excellent attention to detail. For this reason, there are software-testing companies that deliberately recruit people with

---

* What drives winners the most? Is it wanting to achieve the pleasure of victory or avoid the pain of defeat? A lot of people who are successful in sport and in the business world say they don't want to win so much for the winning itself as to avoid the painful experience of losing.

this "disorder." Dyslexics are better at recognizing patterns than non-dyslexics. The British intelligence organization GCHQ specifically looks for dyslexic people to help in the fight against cyberattacks. According to a GCHQ spokesperson, they often excel at unraveling code and analyzing complex problems. They may also be faster to spot patterns and repetitions, and to see what's missing. Director Sir Iain Lobban even said in a speech: "Part of my job is to attract the very best people and harness their talents, and not allow preconceptions and stereotypes to stifle innovation and agility."[9] Even the glorification of one traditional idea of physical beauty is being flipped. The Ugly Models modeling agency in London takes on people who have striking physical characteristics that don't conform to the traditional standards of beauty. And there is strong demand for their clients. It turns out that not every product has to be hawked by beautiful people.

According to the fifth and most recent edition of the *Diagnostic and Statistical Manual of Mental Disorders*, the *DSM-5* (aka the psychiatrists' and psychologists' bible), no fewer than 54 percent of the population suffers from a psychiatric disorder. To me, this is obviously a bizarre conclusion. By adding a range of new "disorders" and lowering the thresholds for existing disorders, the manual evokes the suspicion that it doesn't so much describe insanity as embody it. Wouldn't it be great if a new *DSM* was issued that described our talents rather than our shortcomings? We're making a good beginning, but we've still got a long way to go on this front.

I call the final application of the strategy of reversing the target technique. Let me explain why. A Dutch amateur marksman was on vacation in England, and while out for a walk, he saw a target painted on a tree. There was a bullet hole in the bulls-eye. Nothing too strange about that. But what *was* strange was the fact that there were no other bullet holes at all—neither on the target itself nor anywhere at all on the tree. Someone had obviously hit a perfect bulls-eye in one shot. He was very impressed, as he knew from experience how difficult this was. Not much later, to his amazement he came across an identical target on another tree. How astonishing, to be able to shoot two such perfect bulls-eyes! A bit later he stopped at a pub, and he asked the bartender if he knew anything about an expert marksman in the area, mentioning the targets. The bartender burst out laughing. "We don't have any expert marksmen around here, but we do have a painter. First he shoots a bullet at a tree, then he paints a target around the hole."[10]

The essence of this last method in the strategy of reversing is simple: flip the *order of the process*. Begin at the end, end at the beginning. Here's a simple example: due to her busy social life, a high-school student had a lot of trouble getting her homework done. Her parents (it was her father who shared this story with me) tried everything they could to help her schedule her time better, with all sorts of calendars and efficiency tips. Nothing helped. But then her father flipped the process. He suggested that she start by scheduling her free time. When are you going out? When is that birthday party coming up, and that concert? Because this approach meant that her free time was guaranteed, she was better able to hunker down in the remaining time and make good use of it for studying.[11]

Homeless people often have a very difficult time making their way back to having a home of their own. The typical approach to helping them is to first get them to a shelter, and then often into a group home, where they're generally required to get counseling. A permanent housing situation is provided only once they've demonstrated that they're competent to live independently. But communal living creates all kinds of tensions, and people involved often can't cope with them and head back to the streets. Fortunately, there's another way. Housing First in New York City flipped the problem. They find homeless people permanent housing at the start of assisting them, with no pre-conditions. Their reasoning? Once people have a secure place to live they have peace of mind and can feel the self-respect and sense of autonomy that are crucial to turning all other aspects of their lives around. The approach also means that as opposed to incentivizing change with a promise of a prize in the future, people are offered the more powerful incentive of keeping the good thing they've already got.[12]

From now on, if you are confronted with a problem, ask yourself the question at the heart of this strategy: "Could my problem be the intention?" I think of this as the Miracle Question of Flip Thinking. Ask yourself this question all the time. Before you do anything at all. If you're facing a situation that's harsh, difficult, or oppressive, ask yourself: could a wrong be a right? Could the end be the beginning? Could a disadvantage be an advantage? And then look at reality again through this new frame. Now and then in life you don't have to do anything but reverse a problem into an intention. That's why the strategy of reversing is, when it works, far and away the easiest way to flip-think problems. In essence, you don't have to do anything at all except change your perspective.

PART 3

Finally

In short

A summary of the 15 flip thinking strategies

Strategy 1: Acceptance

What's the strategy? Accept the situation, and see what you can do with it.

What's the effect? A stalemate suddenly turns into a new opportunity.

When do you do it? When reality is unchangeable and inescapable. When resistance is useless. When we have to face the truth. When fooling yourself or others has had its day.

How do you do it? Don't just look at what's immediately visible. Look at underlying trends too (where does it look like this situation is headed?) and actively move in that direction.

Strategy 2: Waiting

What's the strategy? Wait for a new opportunity to come up.

What's the effect? The tide turns after a while. A disadvantage transforms into an advantage, of its own accord. A disaster becomes a blessing.

When do you do it? In two situations: when the circumstances are subject to change, and when you subconsciously need time to incubate an idea.

How do you do it? Keep the "disaster," the "problem," or the "impossibility" in the back of your mind. In the meantime, go for a walk, drink coffee, or take a swim. The opportunity will make itself known, the discovery will come bubbling up of its own accord.

Strategy 3: Amplifying

What's the strategy? Look at what works, and do more of it.

What's the effect? Situations tip like a pair of scales; undergo a metamorphosis, like a caterpillar turning into a butterfly, due to a virtuous circle. Amplification works like a lever.

When do you do it? In three situations: when a situation is unstable or is on the point of taking on a new form, or when a system intervention is possible.

How do you do it? Consistently suppress all inclinations to buy into what doesn't work, look at the things that do work, choose the one that offers the greatest leverage, amplify that one.

Strategy 4: Respect

What's the strategy? The most enjoyable strategy of all. People don't expect to be taken seriously. You show them the consequences of their behavior, attitude, opinions, or desires. You give them what they ask for in so many words. Strangely enough, they usually don't want it.

What's the effect? The situation changes immediately. People instantly ease off. They didn't mean it like that.

When do you do it? When people display contradictory behavior. When they say one thing but do another. Or if they complain but say that everything's okay.

How do you do it? When they complain, say that they've got a point. Tell them you'd be complaining much more if it were you. In short, give them X when they say X.

Strategy 5: Persevering

What's the strategy? The word says it all. Just keep going.

What's the effect? Over time, as long as you persevere, a new opportunity will appear.

When do you do it? As long as you have the feeling that there are still opportunities out there and that you haven't tried everything yet.

How do you do it? Keep trying new ways to achieve your goal. Experiment. Learn by trial and error. Keep your eyes peeled for the unexpected and trust in serendipity.

Strategy 6: Focusing

What's the strategy? Keep your eyes on the goal. What exactly are you trying to achieve? Define your goal as accurately as possible.

What's the effect? You don't have to try harder, instead you develop the power that enables water to slice through steel.

When do you do it? As soon as you want to achieve something.

How do you do it? Let go of what you don't want, forget any interim stages, methods, or conditions, start at the end, what you do want. Keep in mind your ultimate goal and, in the process, keep returning to it. There's nothing wrong with readjusting a goal along the way. Or dropping it.

Strategy 7: Rethinking

What's the strategy? See what the opportunities are. Make up a problem to go with them.

What's the effect? You'll look at the world around you in a different way. There are constant possibilities.

When do you do it? You can use this strategy at almost any time. No question. So much has already been thought up, discovered, attempted, that it would be naive to think that there's nothing of value around that you could put to good use.

How do you do it? Go looking. Google. Talk to people. Research. Ask active questions. Reconsider old ideas that you'd thrown away.

Strategy 8: Eliminating

What's the strategy? Eliminate a part of reality. The part might be either a thing or a thought.

What's the effect? Something that doesn't work anymore moves aside, creating a space. New opportunities arise in that space. The bigger the vacuum, the bigger the force of attraction for new possibilities.

When do you do it? When things don't work anymore. When old beliefs no longer fit the current reality. When we're overloaded.

How do you do it? Eliminate what doesn't work, look at what's left, do something with it.

Strategy 9: Importing

What's the strategy? Get the enemy on board. Make a hacker the head of IT security.

What's the effect? Two birds with one stone. You lose an enemy and gain a loyal ally: he's working for you and dependent on you.

When do you do it? When there's an enemy that you can't beat in the usual ways or with whom you can't collaborate (see no. 10).

How do you do it? Buy, lease, rent the other person.

Strategy 10: Collaborating

What's the strategy? What does the enemy want that you want to do?

What's the effect? A sudden and unexpected alliance.

When do you do it? When the other person wants the same thing you want.

How do you do it? Look for the similarities, emphasize your common interest, forget conflicts (temporarily) and differences of opinion.

Strategy 11: Enticing

What's the strategy? You use the other person's desires to create your own opportunities.

What's the effect? You gain loyal and consistent allies. People who do what they long to do, do so of their own accord, without punishment or threat.

When do you do it? Anywhere that there are people you can use to achieve your goal.

How do you do it? Find out what the other person desires. As people often don't know what they really want, this is often an unexpected approach.

Strategy 12: Flaunting

What's the strategy? Play up what you want to hide. Display the thing you're ashamed of. Show what isn't allowed to be there.

What's the effect? Anxiety vanishes. It's like putting your head in the demon's mouth. Take away the demon's power.

When do you do it? When you conceal something, hide, or suppress it. When you present yourself as better than you actually are.

How do you do it? Play, act, magnify, exaggerate, emphasize, state that you're exaggerating and then exaggerate just a little bit more, turn it into a bit of amateur theater, use bad special effects and sentimental music.

⚊⇄⚊

Strategy 13: Role reversal

What's the strategy? Adopt the other person's behavior, and intensify it.

What's the effect? Disruption of a stuck behavioral pattern. People can no longer play the victim, child, complainant, conscience, or boss, and you're no longer forced to take the opposite role. Taking over their role stops the game and you experience each other as you are.

When do you do it? When people exhibit stuck behavior and expect you to play along in that drama. So: you don't.

How do you do it? By mirroring the other person (in all conceivable ways).

Strategy 14: Disrupting

What's the strategy? Turn all the rules upside down.

What's the effect? Disruption of the existing game. Temporary anarchy. New rules make it possible to play a new game.

When do you do it? When the rules of the game aren't working for you.

How do you do it? Actively investigate which (unwritten) rules are observed. By yourself or by others. Break them.

Strategy 15: Reversing

What's the strategy? Turn a problem into an opportunity. See the good side of misfortune.

What's the effect? The thing that was bothering you suddenly gives you pleasure. A "problem" becomes the "intention."

When do you do it? In a problematic, changeable reality. Don't use it for things that by definition cannot be changed.

How do you do it? Turn the problem into a fact and the fact into an opportunity.

Cast off

The time has come for you to get to work. We've been on a (long) journey together. Now, you've got a summary of the 15 strategies to pop into your pocket for future travels. It's time for you to go it alone. Here are your last-minute instructions.

Flip thinking starts with deciding you want to change something. If a particular "problem" is causing you trouble, from now on don't just think of yourself as a helpless victim. *You* create all the experiences in your universe. You can't change rain, thunder, and lightning, but you *can* change what they mean to you or what you can do with them. In principle, it's simple: you can solve a problem, let it go, or flip-think it. Be sure to make a clear choice.

Use the four questions. What's the problem exactly? (This helps you to identify if you could simply solve it or let it go.) Is it actually a real problem? Are you sure you're not the problem? I think the third question is particularly important. When you want to flip-think a situation, in many cases it's often enough simply to stop stuck thinking. I can't emphasize the power of this variant of flip thinking enough. We often create our own misery, therefore we can also stop doing that. Our problem needs to make it through these first three flip-thinking questions; only then is it suited to the fourth and final question: is the problem the intention? Could we flip-think the problem?

Next, dare to rely on your gut feeling: use your intuition to choose a fundamental attitude. Ask yourself the question: will I approach the situation with love, as work, as a battle, or as a game? Have faith that you can often identify the best fundamental approach intuitively, especially if you have been dealing with a difficult problem for a long time.

Now comes the moment to think it over carefully. Use all the intelligence at your disposal to come up with an action plan, a concrete strategy. Take your time. Be daring, precise, and focused on your plan. Dare to formulate an extremely unorthodox approach if necessary. Write it down, discuss it with other people, give it a trial run, have a dress rehearsal; however you do it, be prepared.

Cast off.

Be decisive. Do it 100 percent and without uncertainty. Uncertainty belongs in the previous step. This phase requires courage, fearlessness, and self-confidence.

Give it time if needed. Each strategy takes a certain amount of time. Sometimes you can flip-think reality like a thunderclap from clear skies, sometimes you need (a lot) more time. A soft-boiled egg takes a matter of minutes, a stew takes hours.

Finally, evaluate. Has the situation been flip-thought? Enjoy!

If not, then just start all over again. Falling's not so bad, but not getting up again is.

Thanks for your attention. I wish you a safe journey. If you'd like to send a message—from home, from a desert island, from a container port or a vibrant tropical city—then I'd really love it. All failures, errors, and successes are more than welcome. You can email us at info@omdenken.nl.

Behind the scenes

Writing a book, that's quite an undertaking.

Fortunately I had a lot of people to help me when I wrote the first edition in 2008. They asked me simple but disruptive questions like "What do you mean?," or wrote "Yaaaaaawn" in the margin in big letters. Without this feedback I would have gone tearing off in the wrong direction.

The first edition was created in two rounds. In the first round, I asked people to use exclamation marks to indicate the sections that they really liked. You could call it the *amplifying* round. I'd like to thank Pepijn Lagerwey, Willem van Boekel, Marieke Frieling, Gijs Nollen, Jan Ruigrok, Daniel Koopmans, Erik F. Kuperus, Bart van der Schaaf, Herberd Prinsen, Rienus Krul, Maartje Kraanen, Johannette van Zoelen, Tim Winkel, Annelies Potuyt, Pieterjan Dwarshuis, and Job Jansen for their exhaustive help. They made comments and suggestions in addition to that, meaning that, after this round, the first contours of the book began to take shape as if by their own accord.

The second round focused on the structure and on getting rid of everything that was weak, mediocre, or "all right." You could call it the *eliminating* round. A number of people were prepared to read the book again with that in mind. I likewise owe them a more than big thank-you. I'd like to thank my friend Jules van Dam (there's a story about him in the book, under the strategy of importing) for his substantive feedback and support in the realization of this book. Thank you to Ruud Tiessen for his fundamental questions and comments about the essence of these scribblings. Finally, in Sebo Ebbens, the man of the spiritual path who has a great sense of humor (fortunately he manages to combine the two things effortlessly), I found an important source of inspiration.

The revised edition has a different background. From previous books I was aware that revising a book is sometimes more complex than writing a new book, just as a major home renovation can be more work than building a new house from scratch. Yet that was exactly the goal. And that's what I did. What a job. Fortunately I was privileged to receive a lot of support during this round too.

I'd like to thank my son, Jan Gunster, for his initiative to revise the book. The decision to produce a fully revised edition was due to his firm conviction that the book was not only due for a design update—he is responsible for all design for Flip Thinking—but for a content update too.

As I wrote in the introduction, an awful lot has happened since 2008. For example, Nelleke Poorthuis has been responsible for establishing our social media (including Facebook and Twitter). The impact of this can't be overstated. Thanks to our online presence, hundreds of people have found us and shared the most inspiring stories. Those stories formed the basis of this revised edition.

I would also like to thank the trainers and actors who produce our shows and workshops day in, day out, for their years of dedication. Thanks to their continuous brainstorming and discussion of the texts, the scenes, and the structure of the programs, the essence of the flip-thinking body of thought has become increasingly clear and more polished over time. The daily practice of the shows and training sessions—for some 15 years now—and constant contact with the public and clients mean that our philosophy is constantly evolving. We teach our participants, but they in turn teach us with their questions, insights, and stories.

Finally, I would like to thank my beloved, my life partner and co-entrepreneur Annemargreet Dwarshuis. Her support was, as always, extremely inspirational and intellectually challenging. The two of us put the finishing touches to this book over two weeks spent in Tenerife. Those weeks were a joy, in every way. Everyone should be so lucky as to experience their life partner as their best co-worker. And after more than 45 years of living and working together. How amazing is that.

Berthold Gunster
Utrecht, 2022

Recommended reading

Gurus, bosses, captains . . .

Creativity

Abrahamson, Eric and David Freedman, *A Perfect Mess: The Hidden Benefits of Disorder* (Orion, 2006)

Anthonio, Gabriël, *Het beste idee van 2013* (Uitgeverij De Wereld, 2014)

Arden, Paul, *It's Not How Good You Are, It's How Good You Want to Be* (Phaidon, 2003)

Arden, Paul, *Whatever You Think, Think the Opposite* (Penguin, 2006)

Bakker, Han, *Creatief denken* (Uitgeverij Nelissen, 1998)

Black, Octavius and Sebastian Bailey, *Mind Gym* (HarperOne, 2014)

Bono, Edward de, *How to Have a Beautiful Mind* (Vermilion, 2004)

Bono, Edward de, *Lateral Thinking* (Penguin, 1970)

Bono, Edward de, *The Mechanism of Mind* (Simon & Schuster, 1969)

Bono, Edward de, *Simplicity* (Penguin, 1998)

Bono, Edward de, *Thinking Course: Powerful Tools to Transform Your Thinking* (MIC Management Resources, 1994)

Boshouwers, Stan, *Handboek voor hemelbestormers* (Uitgeverij Thema, 2005)

Braak, Hans van de, *Ontsnappingskunst* (Amsterdam University Press, 2002)

Busscher, Jeroen, "De kritische mens zit ons in de weg," *De Volkskrant*, May 13, 2006

Byttebier, Igor, *Creativiteit. Hoe? Zo!* (Lannoo, 2002)

Byttebier, Igor and Ramon Vullings, *Creativity Today* (BIS Publishers, 2007)

Claxton, Guy, *Hare Brain, Tortoise Mind: How Intelligence Increases When You Think Less* (Fourth Estate, 1997)

Claxton, Guy and Bill Lucas, *Be Creative: Essential Steps to Revitalize Your Work and Life* (BBC Active, 2004)

Csikszentmihalyi, Mihaly, *Creativity: The Psychology of Discovery and Invention* (Harper Perennial, 2013)

Eastaway, Rob, *Out of the Box: 101 Ideas for Thinking Creatively* (Duncan Baird, 2007)

Fisher, Roger and William Ury, *Getting to Yes: Negotiating an Agreement Without Giving In* (Random House Business Books, 2007)

Florida, Richard, *The Rise of the Creative Class* (Basic Books, 2002)

Gaspersz, Jeff, *Grijp je kans! Vind en benut nieuwe mogelijkheden* (Spectrum, 2009)

Guntern, Gottlieb, *Sieben goldene Regeln der Kreativitätsförderung* (Scalo Zürich, 1999)

Hafkamp, Koos, *Creatief denken* (Academic Service, 2005)

Knoope, Marinus, *De creatiespiraal* (KIC, 1998)

Lewin, Roger, *Complexity: Life at the Edge of Chaos* (University of Chicago Press, 2000)

Maeda, John, *The Laws of Simplicity* (MIT Press, 2006)

Oech, Roger von, *Creative Whack Pack* (card deck), US Games Systems Inc.

Parker, George, *Het grote boek van de creativiteit* (Archipel, 2004)

Pink, Daniel, *Drive* (Riverhead Books, 2009)

Pink, Daniel, *A Whole New Mind* (Riverhead Books, 2005)

Polet, Sybren, *De creatieve factor* (Wereldbibliotheek, 1995)

Trompenaars, Fons, *Creativiteit en innovatie* (Nieuw Amsterdam Uitgevers, 2007)

Psychology and popular psychology

Becker, Gavin de, *The Gift of Fear* (Bantam Doubleday Dell Publishing Group, 1998)

Belitz, Charlene and Meg Lundstrom, *The Power of Flow* (Three Rivers Press, 1999)

Berne, Eric, *Games People Play: The Basic Handbook of Transactional Analysis* (Ballantine Publishing Group, 1964)

Bohm, David, *On Dialogue* (Routledge, 1996)

Cialdini, Robert B., *Influence: Science and Practice* (5th Edition, Allyn & Bacon, 2008)

Cialdini, Robert B. et al., *Yes! 50 Secrets from the Science of Persuasion* (Profile Business, 2007)

Cooperrider, David L. and Diana Whitney, *Appreciative Inquiry: A Positive Revolution in Change* (Berrett-Koehler Publishers, 2005)

Csikszentmihalyi, Mihaly, *Flow* (Harper Perennial, 2008)

Dijksterhuis, Ap, *Het slimme onbewuste* (Uitgeverij Bert Bakker, 2007)

Dijkstra, Pieternel and Gert Jan Mulder, *Overleven in relaties* (Uitgeverij Bert Bakker, 2009)

Fritz, Robert, *The Path of Least Resistance* (Ballantine Books, 1989)

Gladwell, Malcolm, *Blink: The Power of Thinking Without Thinking* (Back Bay Books, 2007)

Gladwell, Malcolm, *The Tipping Point: How Little Things Can Make a Big Difference* (Back Bay Books, 2002)

Goleman, Daniel, *Emotional Intelligence* (Bantam, 2005)

Goleman, Daniel, *Social Intelligence* (Bantam, 2007)

Gottman, John M., *The Seven Principles for Making Marriage Work* (Three Rivers Press, 1999)

Hollander, Jaap and Jeffrey Wijnberg, *Provocatief coachen. De basis* (Scriptum, 2006)

Kahneman, Daniel, *Thinking, Fast and Slow* (Farrar, Straus and Giroux, 2013)

Perel, Esther, *Mating in Captivity* (Harper, 2006)

Rassin, Eric, *Waarom ik altijd gelijk heb: over tunnelvisie* (Scriptum Psychologie, 2007)

Robbins, Anthony, *Awaken the Giant Within* (Simon & Schuster, 2001)

Satir, Virginia, *Making Contact* (Celestial Arts, 1995)

Satir, Virginia, *The New Peoplemaking* (Science and Behavior Books, 1988)

Seligman, Martin E.P., *Authentic Happiness* (Free Press, 2002)

Simons, Daniel J. and Christopher F. Chabris, *Gorillas in Our Midst* (Perception, 1999)

Sitskoorn, Margriet, *Het maakbare brein* (Uitgever Bert Bakker, 2007)

Surowiecki, James, *The Wisdom of Crowds: Why the Many Are Smarter Than the Few and How Collective Wisdom Shapes Business* (Random House, 2004)

Ury, William, *Getting Past No* (Bantam, 1991)

Vonk, Roos, *Ego's en andere ongemakken* (Scriptum Books, 2011)

Waal, Frans de, *The Age of Empathy* (Crown, 2009)

Watzlawick, Paul, *The Situation Is Hopeless But Not Serious* (W.W. Norton, 1993)

Watzlawick, Paul et al., *Change: Principles of Problem Formation and Problem Resolution* (W.W. Norton, 1974)

Wijnberg, Jeffrey, *Gekker dan gek, hoe provocatieve therapie werkt* (Scriptum Psychologie, 2004)

Wijnberg, Jeffrey, *In het diepste van de ziel is niets te vinden* (Scriptum, 2003)

Wijnberg, Jeffrey, *Niemand is iemand zonder de ander* (Scriptum, 2009)

Wiseman, Richard, *Did You Spot the Gorilla?* (Arrow Books, 2004)

Wiseman, Richard, *The Luck Factor* (Miramax, 2003)

Philosophy, spirituality

Cornelis, Arnold, *De vertraagde tijd* (Essence, 1999)

Grün, Anselm, *Buch der Sehnsucht* (Herder, 2003)

Hagen, Steve, *Buddhism Plain and Simple* (Broadway Books, 1998)

Haring, Bas, *De ijzeren wil* (Uitgeverij Houtekiet, 2003)

Haring, Bas, *For a Successful Life* (Beautiful Books, 2008)

Maex, Edel, *Mindfulness* (Lannoo Publishers, 2014)

Taleb, Nassim Nicholas, *Antigrafile* (Random House, 2012)

Taleb, Nassim Nicholas, *The Black Swan* (Random House, 2010)

Tolle, Eckhart, *A New Earth* (Penguin, 2008)

Tolle, Eckhart, *The Power of Now* (New World Library, 1999)

Walsch, Neale Donald, *The Complete Conversations with God* (TarcherPerigee, 2005)

Management, marketing

Becker, Hans Marcel, *Levenskunst op leeftijd* (Eburon, 2003)

Caluwé, Leon de and Hans Vermaak, *Leren veranderen* (Samson, 1999)

Collins, Jim, *Good to Great* (Business Contact, 2004)

Covey, Stephen R., *The 7 Habits of Highly Effective People* (Simon & Schuster, 1989)

Fritz, Robert and Bruce Bodaken, *The Managerial Moment of Truth* (Free Press, 2006)

Godin, Seth, *The Dip* (Portfolio, 2007)

Greene, Robert, *The 48 Laws of Power* (Penguin, 2000)

Groen, Theo et al., *Innoveren, begrippen, praktijk, perspectieven* (Uitgeverij Spectrum, 2006)

Hammond, Sue Annis, *The Thin Book of Appreciative Inquiry* (2nd edition, Thin Book Publishing, 1998)

Hannen, Jos and Kees-Jan van Wees, *Het geroosterde speenvarken en andere managementparabels* (Klapwijk en Keijsers Uitgevers, 2007)

Jackson, Paul and Mark Mckergow, *The Solutions Focus* (Nicholas Brealey, 2006)

Jacobs, Dany, *Strategie, leve de diversiteit* (Pearson Education Benelux, 2005)

Johnson, Sue, *Hold Me Tight* (Little, Brown Spark, 2008)

Kaplan, Sarah and Richard N. Foster, *Creative Destruction: Why Companies That Are Built to Last Underperform the Market* (Doubleday, 2001)

Levitt, Steven D. and Stephen J. Dubner, *Freakonomics* (William Morrow, 2006)

Lindstrom, Martin, *Buyology: Truth and Lies About Why We Buy* (Doubleday, 2008)

Morgan, Gareth, *Images of Organization* (Sage, 1986)

Peters, Tom, *Reimagine! Business Excellence in a Disruptive Age* (Dorling Kindersley, 2006)

Peters, Tom and Robert Waterman, *In Search of Excellence* (HarperBusiness, 2006)

Semler, Ricardo, *The Seven-Day Weekend* (Century, 2004)

Senge, Peter, *The Fifth Discipline* (revised and updated edition, Random House Business Books, 2006)

Senge, Peter et al., *The Dance of Change, The Challenges to Sustaining Momentum in Learning Organizations* (Doubleday, 1999)

Visser, Coert, *Doen wat werkt: Oplossingsgericht werken in organizaties* (Kluwer, 2005)

Visser, Coert and Gwenda Schlundt Bodien, *Paden naar oplossingen* (Just In Time Books, 2008)

Health, happiness

Carter-Scott, Chérie, *If Life Is a Game, These Are the Rules* (Harmony, 1998)

Carter-Scott, Chérie, *If Love Is a Game, These Are the Rules* (Crown Archetype, 1999)

Clifton, Donald O. and Marcus Buckingham, *Now, Discover Your Strengths* (Simon & Schuster, 2001)

Fritz, Robert, *Your Life as Art* (Newfane Press, 2002)

Glouberman, Dina, *The Joy of Burnout* (Skyrons Books, 2013)

Kalse, John, *De kracht van ja* (Ankh-Hermes, 2004)

Katie, Byron, *Loving What Is: Four Questions That Can Change Your Life* (Three Rivers Press, 2003)

Kaufman, Barry Neil, *Son-Rise* (New World Library, 1994)

Richo, David, *The Five Things We Cannot Change* (Shambala, 2006)

Ridder, Willem de, *Handboek spiegologie* (Uitgeverij de Zaak, 1999)

Schaper, Frank, *Geen tijd voor burn-out* (Scriptum Psychologie, 2004)

Segerstrom, Suzanne C., *Breaking Murphy's Law* (The Guilford Press, 2007)

Theater

Brook, Peter, *The Empty Space* (Touchstone, 1995)
Johnstone, Keith, *Impro* (Routledge, 1987)

System theory

Bryan, Bill, Michael Goodman and Jaap Schaveling, *Systeemdenken, ontdekken van onze organizatiepatronen* (Academic Service, 2006)
Choy, Joep, *De vraag op het antwoord: Systemische interventies voor conflicten in organizaties* (Nisto Publicaties, 2005)
Richardson, George, *Feedback Thought* (Pegasus Communications, 1991)
Richardson, George, *Feedback Thought in Social Science and Systems Theory* (University of Pennsylvania Press, 1990)

Notes

Acceptance

1 Jeff Gaspersz, *Grijp je kans! Vind en benut nieuwe mogelijkheden* (Spectrum, 2009)
2 David Richo, *The Five Things We Cannot Change* (Shambala, 2006)
3 John M. Gottman, *The Seven Principles for Making Marriage Work* (Three Rivers Press, 1999)
4 *Psychologie Magazine*, June 2009
5 Byron Katie, *Loving What Is: Four Questions That Can Change Your Life* (Three Rivers Press, 2003)

Observation

1 John Darley and Daniel Batson, " 'From Jerusalem to Jericho': A Study of Situational and Dispositional Variables in Helping Behavior," *Journal of Personality and Social Psychology* 27 (1973): 100–8.
2 Bill Bryan, Michael Goodman, and Jaap Schaveling, *Systeemdenken, ontdekken van onze organisatiepatronen* (Academic Service, 2006)
3 Daniel J. Simons and Christopher F. Chabris, *Gorillas in Our Midst* (Perception, 1999), pp. 1059–74.
4 Guy Claxton, *Hare Brain, Tortoise Mind: How Intelligence Increases When You Think Less* (Fourth Estate, 1997)
5 Daniel Kahneman, *Thinking, Fast and Slow* (Farrar, Straus and Giroux, 2013)

What if everything goes right?

1 Theo Groen et al., *Innoveren, begrippen, praktijk, perspectieven* (Uitgeverij Spectrum, 2006)
2 J. Gardner and A.J. Oswald, "Money and wellbeing," *Journal of Health Economics* 26 (October 2006): 49–60; see also www.vanmaanen.org

Antifragility

1 A. Sagi-Schwartz, M. Bakermans-Kranenburg, S. Linn, and M. van IJzendoorn, "Against All Odds Genocidal Trauma Is Associated with Longer Life-expectancy of the Survivors," *PLoS One* 7 (July 2013)
2 Pamela Weintraub, "The New Survivors," *Psychology Today*, July 2009, https://www.psychologytoday.com/us/articles/200907/the-new-survivors

Stuck thinking

1 Peter Senge, *The Fifth Discipline* (Random House Business Books, 2006)

The four questions

1 Jeffrey Wijnberg, *Niemand is iemand zonder de ander* (Scriptum, 2009)

The strategy of acceptance

1 Roos Vonk, *Ego's en andere ongemakken* (Scriptum, 2011)
2 We heard this story first-hand from the main female character. For privacy reasons the names are not given here.

The strategy of waiting

1 Gabriël Anthonio, *Het beste idee van 2013* (Uitgever De Wereld, 2014)

2 Steven M. Smith and Steven E. Blankenship, "Incubation and the persistence of fixation in problem solving," *American Journal of Psychology* 104/1 (1991): 61–87.

3 Guy Claxton, *Hare Brain, Tortoise Mind: How Intelligence Increases When You Think Less* (Fourth Estate, 1997)

4 Ibid.

The strategy of amplifying

1 Terry S. Trepper et al., "Steve de Shazer and the Future of Solution Based Therapy," *Journal of Marital and Family Therapy*, May 2007, https://onlinelibrary.wiley.com/doi/abs/10:1111/j.1752-0606:2006.tb01595.

2 *Algemeen Dagblad*, Thema section, May 19, 2008

3 The quote is a personal communication by Martin Seligman, noted down by Louis Cauffman; source: Louis Cauffman, *Simpel, oplossingsgerichte positieve psychologie in actie* (Boom-Lemma, 2013)

4 Tom Peters, *Business Excellence in a Disruptive Age* (Dorling Kindersley, 2006)

5 David L. Cooperrider and Diana Whitney, *Appreciative Inquiry: A Positive Revolution in Change* (Berrett-Koehler Publishers, 2005)

6 Eric Rassin, *Waarom ik altijd gelijk heb* (Scriptum Psychologie, 2007)

7 *De Volkskrant*, section Hart en Ziel, May 21, 2008

8 Arie Nouwen, "Een stuk papier vouwen om de Maan te bereiken," astroblogs, 1 September 2009, www.astroblogs.nl/2009/09/01/een-stuk-papier-vouwen-om-de-maan-te-bereiken

The strategy of respect

1 The story comes from Jan Ruigrok.
2 Kirsten Ronda, "Feliciteer ouders met scheldende kinderen," *Pedagogiek in Praktijk*, November 27 2014, www.pedagogiek.nu/feliciteer-ouders-met-scheldende-kinderen/1025959
3 *Der Spiegel*, November 17 2011, www.spiegel.de/international/zeitgeist/this-is-a-oh-never-mind-kids-thwart-robbery-with-piggy-banks-a-798372.html
4 ZDF News, January 17 2012
5 The story was told by John Cleese various times in autumn 2014, including on *The Graham Norton Show*, 10 October 2014.
6 With thanks to Jan Ruigrok, who noted down this story from the radio for me.

The strategy of persevering

1 Edel Maex, *Mindfulness* (Lannoo Publishers, 2014)
2 Steve de Shazer and Yvonne Dolan, *More Than Miracles: The State of the Art of Solution-Focused Brief Therapy* (Routledge, 2007)
3 J.G. March, "The technology of foolishness," in J.G. March and J.P. Olsen (eds), *Ambiguity and Choice in Organizations* (Bergen: Universitetsforlaget, 1979), pp. 69–81.
4 W. Mischel, Y. Shoda, and M.L. Rodriguez, "Delay of Gratification in Children," *Science* 244 (1989): 933–8.

The strategy of focusing

1 Gabriël Anthonio, *Het beste idee van 2013* (Uitgeverij De Wereld, 2014)
2 Paul Arden, *Whatever You Think, Think the Opposite* (Penguin, 2006)
3 Marc Mangel and Francisco J. Samaniego, "Abraham Wald's Work on Aircraft Survivability," *Journal of the American Statistical Association*, Vol. 79, Issue 386 (1984): 259–67.

4 Suzanne C. Segerstrom, *The Glass Half-Full* (Robinson, 2009)

5 Suzanne C. Segerstrom, *Breaking Murphy's Law* (The Guilford Press, 2007)

6 Coert Visser and Gwenda Schlundt Bodien, *Paden naar oplossingen* (Just In Time Books, 2008)

The strategy of rethinking

1 Richard Wiseman, *Did You Spot the Gorilla?* (Arrow Books, 2004)

The strategy of eliminating

1 Sarah Kaplan and Richard N. Foster, *Creative Destruction: Why Companies That Are Built to Last Underperform the Market* (Doubleday, 2001)

2 Martien Bouwmans, ING via Aukje Nauta, Factor Vijf

3 George Parker, *Het grote boek van de creativiteit* (Archipel, 2004)

4 *The New York Times*, August 30, 2012, https://www.nytimes.com/2012/08/31/nyregion/mta-expands-an-effort-to-remove-trash-cans.html

5 DutchNews.NL, November 2008, https://www.dutchnews.nl/news/2008/11/stand-up_meetings_would_cut_co/

6 With thanks to Katrien Heere, one of the parents involved, who sent us this story.

7 Jeff Gaspersz, *Grijp je kans! Vind en benut nieuwe mogelijkheden* (Spectrum, 2009)

The strategy of importing

1 Joep Wennekers, "Takeovers at gun-point: Does hostility pay off in the long-run?," Master's thesis, Radboud University (2021), https://theses.ubn.ru.nl/bitstream/handle/123456789/11044/Wennekers%2C_Joep_1.pdf?sequence=1

2 *Guardian*, November 18, 2014, https://www.theguardian.com/world/2014/nov/18/neo-nazis-tricked-into-raising-10000-for-charity

The strategy of collaborating

1 William Ury, *Getting Past No* (Bantam, 1991)
2 Web Urbanist, April 2013, https://weburbanist.com/2013/04/30/symbiotic-design-life-saving-meds-hide-in-spare-space/
3 This story was sent to us by Jan de Kruif, the builder in question.
4 For reasons of privacy, the names of the people and company concerned are not given here.
5 This story was told to us by Erika de Roo. It is her own story.
6 William Ury, *Getting Past No* (Bantam, 1991)
7 This story was told to us by Liesbeth Ligtenberg.
8 Octavius Black and Sebastian Bailey, *Mind Gym* (HarperOne, 2014)
9 BBC News, June 28, 2013, https://www.bbc.co.uk/news/uk-england-hereford-worcester-23104502

The strategy of enticing

1 Anselm Grün, *Buch der Sehnsucht* (Herder, 2003)
2 Robert B. Cialdini, *Influence: Science and Practice* (5th edition, Allyn & Bacon, 2008)
3 M. Hewstone, J. Harwoord, A. Voice, and J. Kenworthy, "Intergroup Contact and Grandparent-Grandchild Communication: The Effects of Self-Disclosure on Implicit and Explicit Biases Against Older People," *Group Processes & Intergroup Relations*, 9/3 (2006): 413–29.
4 Pieternel Dijkstra and Gert Jan Mulder, *Overleven in relaties* (Uitgeverij Bert Bakker, 2009)
5 This story was sent to us by Nicolet Mulder.
6 Robert B. Cialdini, *Influence: Science and Practice* (5th edition, Allyn & Bacon, 2008)
7 Robert Cialdini et al., *Yes! 50 Secrets from the Science of Persuasion* (Profile Business, 2007)
8 Eric Abrahamson and David Freedman, *A Perfect Mess: The Hidden Benefits Of Disorder* (Orion, 2006)

The strategy of flaunting

1 Martin Lindstrom, *Buyology: Truth and Lies About Why We Buy* (Doubleday, 2008)

2 *The Scotsman*, September 2011, https://www.scotsman.com/arts-and-culture/interview-stephen-merchant-comedian-1659794

The strategy of role reversal

1 Said by a couple regarding their children in an episode of Dutch soap opera *Goede Tijden, Slechte Tijden*.

2 This story is from Esther de Graaf.

3 This story is from Martine van Eijk.

The strategy of disrupting

1 The term "seesawing" was introduced to neuro-linguistic programming (NLP) by Anneke Meijer and Paul Bindels, who made a note of the approach based on Frank Farrelly's working method; source: Jaap Hollander & Jeffrey Wijnberg, *Provocatief coachen. De basis* (Scriptum, 2006).

2 Gareth Morgan, *Images of Organization* (Sage, 1986)

3 Robert Fritz, *Your Life as Art* (Newfane Press, 2002)

4 Edward de Bono, *Sur/petition: The New Business Formula to Help You Stay Ahead of the Competition* (Vermilion, 2019)

5 This story is from John Swaneveld.

6 "HEMA top 5 shoplifted products," CCCP, March 2, 2010, https://staatsloterij-cccp.blogspot.com/2010/03/hema-top-5-shoplifted-products.html

7 *De Volkskrant*, Kennis section, October 11, 2008, p. 7.

The strategy of reversing

1 Mark Twain, *The Adventures of Tom Sawyer* (American Publishing Company, 1876)

2 Richard Wiseman, *Did You Spot the Gorilla?* (Arrow Books, 2004)

3 Nassim Nicholas Taleb, *Antigrafile* (Random House, 2012)

4 Virginia Satir, *Making Contact* (Celestial Arts, 1995)

5 This story is from Dagmar Ruth Bouwman.

6 Bill Bryson, *Made in America* (Transworld Publishers, 1998)

7 Frans de Waal, *The Age of Empathy* (Crown, 2009)

8 Gavin de Becker, *The Gift of Fear* (Bantam Doubleday Dell Publishing Group, 1998)

9 Speech at the University of Leeds, October 4, 2012, https://www.gchq.gov.uk/speech/director-gchq-makes-speech-in-tribute-to-alan-turing

10 J. Hannen and K.-J. van Wees, *Het geroosterde speenvarken en andere managementparabels* (Klapwijk en Keijsers Uitgevers, 2007)

11 The story was told to us by Bert van Baar, the father in question.

12 The initial Housing First success rates are extremely encouraging. Research shows that around 85 percent of participants have been able to keep their homes long-term. Following the New York example, similar projects have commenced in various cities across the US and Canada. In the Netherlands, the Housing First principle has been implemented by Discus in Amsterdam and De Tussenvoorziening in Utrecht.

Index

ABOUT THE AUTHOR

Berthold Gunster (1959) is the founder of the Omdenken philosophy.
After studying at the Theatre Academy in Utrecht he worked as a theater
director and writer for years. He also created projects like *Not Your Mama's
Bus Tour* with homeless people in Chicago and *Why Is Stas Addicted?* in
Ukraine.

Since 2001 he and his team have been offering training, workshops, and
shows about Omdenken to companies and individuals in any imaginable
place in the Netherlands, as well as in Germany, Belgium, Spain, the UK,
France, Greece, Switzerland, Singapore, and many other places.

Berthold has written 13 bestsellers about the Omdenken theory, selling
over a million copies in the Netherlands. His work is translated into various languages.

Twitter: @BertholdGunster

What is Omdenken?

Omdenken is the Dutch art of flip thinking. It's the art of turning problems into opportunities. It will help you think in terms
of possibilities and chances, instead of limitations and threats. It
encourages you to stop saying yes-but to life. And start saying yes-and.

Omdenken is a company based in Utrecht, the Netherlands. The company has about 10 people working in the office, and 15 very dedicated free-
lance trainers, actors, and technicians.

omdenken.com

Omdenken and the Omdenken logo are registered trademarks in Europe,
the UK, and the USA. The use of our logo, copying any of our spoken and
written text, lyrics, or ideas, or selling workshops and lectures is not allowed
without prior written approval by the Omdenken company.

Omdenken B.V.
Oudegracht 263, 3511 NM Utrecht, The Netherlands
+31 30 2334062   info@omdenken.nl